THE FOOL'S
GUIDE TO

Tarot

THE FOOL'S GUIDE TO

Tarot

A No-Nonsense Guide to Tarot Reading and Understanding Tarot Card Meanings

MYSTIC RAINN

CORAL GABLES

Cover Design: Roberto Núñez
Cover Photo/illustrations: Adobe Stock
Layout & Design: Roberto Núñez

For permission requests, please contact the publisher at:
Mango Publishing Group
2850 S Douglas Road, 2nd Floor
Coral Gables, FL 33134 USA
info@mango.bz

For special orders, quantity sales, course adoptions and corporate sales, please email the publisher at sales@mango.bz. For trade and wholesale sales, please contact Ingram Publisher Services at customer.service@ingramcontent.com or +1.800.509.4887.

The Fool's Guide to Tarot: A No-Nonsense Guide to Tarot Reading and Understanding Tarot Card Meanings

Library of Congress Cataloging-in-Publication number: 2024941531
ISBN: (print) 978-1-68481-459-6, (ebook) 978-1-68481-461-9
BISAC category code OCC024000, BODY, MIND & SPIRIT / Divination / Tarot

Printed in the United States of America

To my mother, who has already transcended this earthly realm.
Look, Ma! I wrote a book!

Table of Contents

A Letter to My Dear Fool

My dear Fool,

They say that when the student is ready, the teacher will appear. Some of you may have been led to this book by fate, receiving it as a gift or stumbling upon it during a conversation with a friend. But often, people start their journey with tarot as a solo traveler. A lone student who has picked up a deck of cards or a tarot book in secret. Regardless of how you found your way here, I am deeply honored to be your guide as you delve into the ancient art of tarot—a practice with the potential to change your life forever.

I am struck by the realization that I, too, am a lifelong student who has somehow become a teacher, and I am excited by the opportunity to step into this role. I never imagined myself in the role of a teacher, but as I reflect on my journey with tarot, I realize that each of us has the potential to become both a student and a teacher, continuously learning and growing as we navigate the mysteries of life.

I hope that as we embark on this adventure together, we can not only learn tarot but also uncover deeper truths about ourselves and gain a better understanding of the world around us. And so, with an open heart and a sense of wonder, I embrace this opportunity to share my knowledge with you, knowing that we are all on this journey together.

For a year, I dedicated myself to crafting this book with care, knowing its words may have a lasting impact on those who read them, and it is a responsibility that I do not take lightly. My aspiration is that through

this process, we can complete the quote that I started this letter
to you with:

"They say that when the student is ready, the teacher will appear...
When the student is truly ready, *the teacher will disappear.*"

Let the journey begin!

Welcome to the Fool's Journey!

Welcome, my dear Fools and seekers of ancient wisdom, to your new Fool's Journey! If you have stumbled upon this book, then you are probably on a quest to unlock the secrets of tarot—a mystical tool that dances between the here and now and future possibilities. This is not your typical tarot guide filled with esoteric jargon, as I have taken it upon myself to embrace creative liberty and employ some unique tactics to help with memorization. I aspire to untangle definitions that are usually heavily convoluted and offer a more straightforward approach to tarot. This book is meant to de-mystify the mystical, making this spiritual practice more accessible to everyone.

The road to learning tarot is long. Trust me, I know. I have paid for countless tarot courses, both in-person and virtual, attended tarot seminars, and joined tarot groups and community forums, all in pursuit of a mentor who could explain tarot to me. Alas, I found none. I never found someone who could teach tarot to me in a way that I could easily understand. Eventually, I gave up on that route and committed to self-study.

Frustration led me to the sacred basement of a Costa Coffee in London, and I thank Goddess for that one table in the corner that no one ever sat at except me. This is where I would bury myself in the countless tarot books that I purchased, flipping through never-ending pages. I got to highlighting and writing notes in the margins while comparing each piece of literature for accuracy. Oh, it was a painstaking process, but when I finally figured out the system of tarot, I said to myself that one day I would make the process easier for someone else. So here I am now, making it easier (hopefully) for you and bridging the gap between the arcane and the accessible. Do not get me wrong—you will still need a lot of patience and a highlighter for this, but trust the process.

But why listen to me? Because, my dear Fool, I will give it to you straight without the mystical babbling. This book is about removing the fluff and getting to the point. There is not going to be any elaborate advice written in a sing-song tone on how to connect with *energy*. How come? Because I am not your stereotypical spiritual teacher, I am a straight-talking Black woman from Queens. You will not find me meditating on mountain tops due to my disinterest in climbing them, and you will not catch me cleansing crystals as I have probably (definitely) misplaced them. But if you are here, flipping through these pages, then we already have something in common, and I like you.

Now, for my qualifications—what makes me the one to guide you through your Fool's Journey of tarot? Well, not to alarm anyone, but I talk to dead people and come with a fair amount of psychic abilities. Yes, you read that right. It is also not because I signed up for some psychic masterclass either. My abilities kicked in when my dead sister paid me an unexpected visit and politely asked (aggressively demanded) that I assist her with some unfinished business. But when it comes to you, do not fret, my dear Fool, as learning to read tarot does not mean that you will start holding seances for departed souls, unless, of course, that is your thing. In tarot, you will be having conversations with yourself or the person you are reading for.

Grab your tarot deck (a Rider-Waite-Smith tarot deck, please) and let us unpack this system one card at a time.

Part I

The Basics

CHAPTER 1

The Fool's Guide to Tarot

The History of Tarot

The history of tarot draws a lot of controversy and like the cards themselves, it is clouded in mystery regarding its origin. This mystery has attracted many mystics, spiritual seekers, and scholars for over a century. Due to this, there are many interpretations and varying narratives about its historical background, creating a situation where a lot of the accounts are speculation and myth. For this book, we will discuss the most popular accounts of where the tarot came from.

Contrary to a lot of other ancient traditions, tarot does not have a clear-cut lineage and does not derive from a specific moment of inception. Instead, there has been a slow emergence over time, and its appearance in society has grown, spanning different geographical regions throughout the centuries as aspects of it have found their way intertwined in various philosophies and mystical traditions. These various appearances have created a dynamic, causing people to piecemeal its origin story.

The most prevalent theory suggests that tarot has Italian beginnings and originated in fifteenth-century Northern Italy, where the cards allegedly were originally designed as a deck of playing cards. A popular deck known as the Visconti-Sforza deck is widely known as being one of the oldest tarot decks made in the 1400s and carries symbolic imagery many believe alludes to esoteric meanings. It is said that this deck was used for playing an Italian card game known as tarocchini, but whether the tarot deck as a whole was created for card games or to be used as a divination tool is still the subject of continued debate.

Another theory suggests that tarot derived from ancient Egyptian mysticism and that the symbolism depicted in the tarot deck mirrors the esoteric knowledge passed down from Egyptian teachings with the Major Arcana of tarot acting as a visual depiction of the soul's spiritual evolution. Additionally, it has been claimed the tarot may also have German, Austrian, French, or Romani influence; however, this is speculation due to the lack of historical evidence.

There was an explosion of interest in tarot in the nineteenth century due to the rise of the occult and secret societies. The Hermetic Order of the Golden Dawn, which was founded in 1887, played a crucial role in tarot due to it adding additional concepts to the practice such as the kabbalah, astrology, and alchemy. Fast-forward to the twentieth century and Carl Jung added his influence by suggesting that the cards were archetypal symbols that offered insight into the collective unconscious and to the depths of the human psyche. This impacted tarot's influence in the occult by expanding its use to consist of being a tool for personal and spiritual exploration.

While no one knows for certain the origins of tarot, what is certain is that the symbolism in tarot has evolved over the centuries to include new or updated meanings that are relevant to the current times, often to reflect changing cultural, social, and linguistic contexts. Each revival of tarot contributes to the further expansion and reinterpretation of its visual language, as signs and symbols can sometimes take on new meanings due to the continued evolution of culture and language.

Today, modern tarot has become a versatile instrument that people use to seek guidance and creative inspiration while using it as a method of self-discovery. With each new deck published, artists and creators add to the interpretation of tarot's visual language as culture and language continue to evolve. This allows tarot to remain relevant and accessible catering to diverse tastes and spiritual practices. While the history of tarot remains controversial, all theories contribute to the craft and each evolution highlights why it, as a tool, is covered in mystique. Whether created in Italy or elsewhere, tarot is used for divination, contemplation, or self-discovery, and persists as a timeless mirror reflecting the depths of the human experience.

The Importance of the Rider-Waite-Smith Tarot

The Rider-Waite-Smith tarot deck is the deck you need to know how to read. The imagery of this deck is also the imagery you will learn in this book. Why do you need to know how to read it? Because, my dear Fool, every tarot deck that is produced today is based on this deck. Some new decks may have imagery added due to the creator's interpretation, but make no mistake, it is highly likely that the creator started with this deck first, which then influenced the deck that they created. This deck has become the educational foundation of tarot reading and equips readers with a universal understanding of tarot symbols. If you learn how to read this deck, then you can read any deck that you can get your hands on (money-back not guaranteed).

The Rider-Waite-Smith tarot deck, often abbreviated as the RWS deck, is one of the most prominent decks in the world of tarot, and the imagery of tarot often seen in pop culture, such as movies, books, and art, usually originates from this deck. This deck is like the Beyoncé of the ancient divination world—iconic and influential.

Being more than a century old, the RWS deck was initially published in 1910. Renowned occultist and member of the Hermetic Order of the Golden Dawn Arthur Edward Waite collaborated with artist and fellow member of the Golden Dawn Pamela Colman Smith, known affectionately as "Pixie," and brought the modern-day tarot deck to life. As members of the Order, both Waite and Smith had a deep understanding of occult symbolism, which was translated through Smith's artistry ultimately infusing the deck with its imagery. This deck is one of the most accessible decks for beginners as Smith's imagery is clear and abundant with symbolism providing visual cues that help with interpretation and memorization. It established a set of standardized tarot imagery due to the detailed scenes in both the Major and Minor Arcana, which created a visual narrative that tarot readers use today.

Oh! And who was "Rider," some of you may ask? It was the name of the original publisher, the Rider Company.

Traditional Tarot versus Intuitive Tarot

Traditional tarot reading and intuitive tarot reading are two different approaches to interpreting tarot cards and these approaches have fundamental differences. This book will teach you traditional tarot, not intuitive tarot—well, the CliffsNotes version of it anyway, because nobody has time to be here all day. Traditional tarot reading follows a set system and card interpretations are based on the original intended meanings of the cards. Why is traditional tarot important? Because when you are starting your spiritual journey, your intuition has not fully kicked in yet! Studying this book will help you learn the system of tarot even as a beginner with no background information or intuitive ability. I always found it annoying when tarot teachers—I have had many—would say to me in a sing-song voice, "*Look at the card. What do you* feel?" **Um, ma'am, I don't know! Like homeboy on the horse is riding through the death card, and you're asking me how I feel?! I gotta tell you, Susan, not great!**

When you are new to tarot, daunting cards that you do not understand, such as Death, are enough to cause anxiety. Not only may you not understand the card because you are still learning, but your mind is also now jumping to conclusions on what the meaning *may* be. You start asking yourself, "Is someone dying?!" "Oh my God, is my relationship over?!" (probably) "Am I overthinking this or is this my intuition kicking in?!" It is for this reason that this book will not ask you to read tarot based on your intuition and instead will spare you the confusion by giving you the actual definition of the cards.

As mentioned before, traditional tarot reading follows an established system. The tarot deck that is used today was made with a specific intention and the card meanings are deliberate. These meanings have been passed down through generations of tarot readers, and they are often based on a combination of historical symbolism and esoteric knowledge. Traditional tarot reading also heavily relies on tarot card spreads (more on that later) and specific positions within the spread to provide insight and answers. On the other hand, intuitive tarot reading is more fluid and flexible as it relies heavily on the reader's developed intuitive abilities to interpret meanings. Because intuitive ability and inner guidance are different from person to person, an intuitive tarot reading may not adhere to the traditional meanings of the cards.

Both traditional and intuitive tarot reading approaches have their merits and can provide valuable insights; however, learning traditional tarot will help ease a beginner into the craft, even if their intuition is still in the process of developing.

CHAPTER 2

The Fool's Guide to Using This Book

How to Read This Book

The structure of this book aims to streamline your learning experience and enhance your understanding of the tarot deck. By breaking down each card into specific sections, you are offered a holistic view of its symbolism, meaning, and how it applies to the real world. Here is how to use each section:

Title
Start by reading the title of the card to familiarize yourself with its name and imagery. Each card is assigned a title to jog your memory and serve as a helpful reference point during readings.

Astrological Associations
Review the astrological associations to understand the cosmic influences at play. Understanding the astrological influences connected to each card adds depth to your interpretations. This knowledge expands your understanding and allows for more nuanced readings.

Keywords
Take note of the keywords to grasp the main concept of the card. These words encapsulate the essence of the card, providing a quick reference

for its main themes and symbolism. They can also be used as handy cues during readings or journaling sessions.

Understanding the Card

This section explores the card's symbolism, meaning, and significance within its historical and cultural contexts.

Card Meaning

Here, you'll find a detailed explanation of the card's definition and implications, along with teachable moments that you can apply to real-world scenarios.

Affirmation

Embrace the affirmations to harness the power of intention and manifestation, helping you to align with the energy of the card and draw positive experiences into your life.

Journal Prompts

Each chapter concludes with a set of journal prompts designed to deepen your connection with the card and promote self-reflection. These prompts encourage you to explore the card's significance in your life, uncover hidden insights, and set intentions for personal growth and transformation.

Suggested Study Materials

Rider-Waite-Smith Tarot Deck

Not to beat a dead horse, but this one is not suggested. It is required.

Notebook

Your Fool's Journey of learning how to read tarot deserves a dedicated space to write down your interpretations and personal insights. I suggest you use a notebook for your notes and your scribbles in the margins, as well as for a personal tarot journal where you answer the journal prompts you will be given for each card. Using a notebook in this way will help you create a deeper understanding of the card meanings and increase your connection to the cards over time.

Index Cards

For those of you who prefer a more interactive approach, consider creating flashcards that summarize the key meanings of each tarot card on one side and challenge yourself to recall those meanings on the other side of the flashcard.

Pen/Pencil

These ink-filled delights are your tools of engagement. Use them to underline and actively interact with the information in this book. I promise you I will not be offended. Add a little doodle if you must.

Highlighter

There is nothing wrong with a pop of color; in fact, I highly recommend it. Use a highlighter to transform this book into your personal tarot visual study guide. I suggest using different colors to categorize information like keywords, card meanings, and personal reflections, making the information easier to remember.

Study Tips

Keywords Are Your Friend

This book is filled with keywords, and I suggest you use them. Each keyword is a simplified card definition and is meant to jog your memory making it easier to recall the meaning of each card.

Meet the Royal Family

Unlike traditional teaching methods that may rely solely on memorization, "The Royal Family" is a teaching method I created meant to offer a more relatable and memorable way to connect with the court cards. Its framework will better help you understand the characteristics, energies, and roles the court cards play in your tarot readings.

Daily One-Card Tarot Readings

Congratulations! You are the lucky winner that has just been assigned daily homework (you are welcome, of course). Learning how to read tarot cards requires more than understanding the theory behind each card. It is important to give yourself or a trusted guinea pig a daily one-card reading. This practice will give you hands-on reading experience turning you into that tarot reader you aspire to be. Afterall, that is why you are here, right?

Create a Tarot Journal

Write about your daily one-card tarot readings, reflect on the circumstances surrounding each reading, and make notes of your thoughts or emotions that a reading provoked. By keeping a tarot journal, you can revisit your experiences and observe how your insights evolve over time.

Consistency

Put aside time each day for your tarot practice. It is important to stay consistent to help with developing a deep understanding of the cards and remembering tarot card meanings.

Patience, Patience, Patience!

Learning how to read tarot is a Fool's Journey. Be patient with yourself and let go of the idea that you will remember every tarot card meaning the first time (although, if you do, kudos!). Embrace the process of gradual understanding and know that it is okay to refer to this book as often as required.

CHAPTER 3

The Fool's Guide to the Tarot Deck

This chapter requires you to have the patience and the highlighter I told you to have at the beginning of the book. Remember the "Welcome to the Fool's Journey" section that you "forgot" to read?

So, what is this mystical thing we call tarot? Well, for starters, it is paper and ink. Nothing more. Nothing less. If you want to get technical, it is a stack of papers. I say this to emphasize the amount of power the deck does not have by itself. The power and the magic come from *you*. Oftentimes, when people pick up a tarot deck for the first time, they assume that they have picked up a magical object, but without a reader, a tarot deck is about as useful as a magic wand without its wizard.

Let us address some other misconceptions and frequently asked questions I have received during the duration of my time as a tarot reader.

Do Tarot Cards Predict the Future?

Oh, my dear Fool, if only life were that simple! Tarot cards offer guidance and insights, but they cannot predict your winning lottery numbers or the name of your future spouse. That is a job for the Universe's personal assistant, not a deck of cards. If it could predict winning lottery numbers, I would not be writing this book and instead would be swimming in cash somewhere in Bora Bora.

Can Tarot Control Your Fate?

Sorry, but we are not handing out magic wands here. Tarot can provide guidance, but it will not rewrite your destiny. The real power lies in your choices and actions, not in a deck of cards. So, put on your big boss pants and take charge of your life.

Is Tarot Evil?

No! Tarot cards are just pieces of cardstock with cool pictures printed in ink on them. If anything, they are more likely to summon a craving for chocolate than any dark forces. So, grab your snacks, relax, and let us dive into the magical world of tarot without any unnecessary exorcisms, okay? I promise you that you have not just opened a portal to the *"unknown."* Also, *no*, you will not go to hell (shoutout to my churchgoers!).

Does Reading Tarot Require Special Powers?

Oh, my dear Fool, the only superpower you need is the ability to shuffle the cards and for you butterfingers out there that have a tough time shuffling, you can mix the cards in a hat and pull them out one by one. Tarot is about connecting with your inner wisdom, not summoning your childhood pet goldfish (the one you forgot to feed) from another dimension.

Can Only Psychics Read Tarot?

I hate to burst your bubble, but you do not need a crystal ball or a psychic hotline to read tarot cards. You just need an open mind, a sense of curiosity, and maybe a cup of tea—or something stronger if you prefer. Tarot is for anyone willing to embrace their inner intuitive badass in the making.

Is Tarot Reading about Dark Stuff?

Tarot is not all doom and gloom. Yes, we might encounter the occasional Tower card letting you know that your current situation might start crumbling down, but there is also plenty of sunshine in tarot as well. Tarot is like life—a mix of light and shadows.

Now that the elephant in the room has been addressed and we have discussed what tarot is *not*, let us now talk about what tarot *is*.

The Fool's Journey

Study Tip: The Fool's Journey describes the meaning of tarot. Read carefully.

Welcome to the enthralling expedition known as the Fool's Journey!

Tarot is a depiction of the Fool's Journey and is a tool to assess where the Fool is on the journey at any given time. The Fool's Journey is a metaphor that represents embracing life's adventures, lessons, and both of its gifts and challenges. This symbolic journey is a reminder that life is a constant voyage of growth and exploration. It is a journey that is undertaken by the Fool, who travels through the tarot deck, encountering different life experiences along the way as it works to reach the end of its expedition.

As the Fool progresses through the tarot deck, they encounter a series of archetypal characters and significant life events that shape their journey through life. Each tarot card represents a unique lesson, challenge, or revelation that contributes to the Fool's growth and expansion. Through the Fool's Journey, they learn that they must confront their fears, embrace their passions, and navigate the outcomes of their choices.

Throughout the journey, the Fool learns the importance of balance, patience, trust, and embracing the unknown. They experience various situations that challenge their deeply held beliefs, face moments of deep self-reflection, and, as a result, emerge from the journey wiser and more self-aware. The journey teaches the Fool to approach life with curiosity, courage, and a willingness to take risks. It reminds the Fool to listen to their intuition, trust the unfolding of their path even if it cannot be seen, and view lessons as opportunities for growth.

Now, who is the Fool, you may ask? It is *you,* my dear.

Study Tip: Because the Fool is traveling through the tarot, the tarot deck itself is a picture documentary (pictorial) explaining the Fool's Journey. If you line up the cards in order, they form a story.

The Structure of a Tarot Deck

A tarot deck consists of seventy-eight cards made up of two main components: the Major Arcana and the Minor Arcana. Together, these two components form a comprehensive framework that captures the essence of the human experience and provides insights into various aspects of life.

Understanding the Major Arcana

These bad boys—and girls—are the rockstars of the tarot deck, strutting around with their larger-than-life personalities and epic tales to tell. Think of them as the A-listers of the tarot realm, here to drop wisdom bombs and shake up your cosmic cocktail. These cards mean business! They represent the big stuff in life, the game-changers, the "hold onto your seat, it's about to get real" moments. We are talking about the highs, lows, curveballs, and wake-up calls that life loves to throw at us.

The Major Arcana, which is often referred to as the "trump cards," is comprised of twenty-two archetypal cards that represent significant milestones and *major* themes that typically occur in life. Each card in the Major Arcana embodies a distinct energy and story, and refers to key life lessons and events.

The Major Arcana cards are also known as the "trump cards" due to their elevated status and *major* influence within the tarot deck. The term "trump" originates from card games, where certain cards hold a higher rank and power over others.

WHY DO MAJOR ARCANA CARDS HOLD SO MUCH POWER?

Archetypes

Each card in the Major Arcana represents an archetype or universal symbol that resonates with the collective human experience.

Universal Themes

The Major Arcana cards encompass a wide range of universal themes such as success, money, love, faith, and personal transformation. These themes speak to individual circumstances and to the broader human experience.

Symbolism

Each card in the Major Arcana embodies deep symbolism and energy that represents a significant life theme.

Key Milestones

The Major Arcana represents the crucial turning points and milestones in one's life.

Significance

The Major Arcana cards carry a heavier influence in a reading. When a Major Arcana card appears, it often signifies a significant event, a major shift in life path, or a crucial lesson that will hold great significance in one's life.

> **Study Tip:** Identifying the cards—Major Arcana cards have keywords at the bottom of the card and are numbered zero to twenty-one.

Understanding the Minor Arcana

Let us dive into the Minor Arcana, the support crew of the tarot deck! These fifty-six little rascals (cards) may not have the glitz and glam of the Major Arcana, but trust me, they are the unsung heroes that keep the tarot train chugging along.

Picture this: the Minor Arcana is like your trusty sidekick, always there to add a splash of flavor and a little drama to your readings. These cards may not have the big personalities of their Major Arcana cousins, but what they lack in glamor, they make up for in practicality and everyday shenanigans. The Minor Arcana consists of fifty-six cards that represent the nitty gritty details and individual moments within a major life event. These cards portray the more mundane aspects of daily life by giving you all the juicy details.

These cards are not here to blow your mind with cosmic revelations like the Major Arcana or to predict the winning lottery numbers (again, sorry folks); their job is more down-to-earth. They are all about spilling the tea of daily life as well as the tea on your relationships, career, emotions, and the good ol' material world.

THE SUITS AND ELEMENTS

The Minor Arcana is divided into four suits: Wands, Cups, Swords, and Pentacles. These suits represent distinct aspects of the human experience and are associated with the four classical elements: fire, water, air, and earth.

Each suit in the Minor Arcana consists of ten numbered cards (Ace to Ten) and four court cards (Page, Knight, Queen, and King). The numbered cards depict the details of everyday situations, and the court cards represent people with distinct personalities and roles that might appear in everyday situations.

> **Study Tip:** Identifying the cards—Minor Arcana cards have the suit at the bottom of the card and are numbered Ace to Ten.

Wands (Fire)

The suit of Wands is associated with the element of fire (wands look like matchsticks). Wands and fire represent the energy of drive, ambition, passion, movement, creativity, and the spark (think of fire) of inspiration.

> **Study Tip:** Wands represent your passions!

Cups (Water)

The suit of Cups is associated with the element of water (cups hold water). The Cups and water represent emotions, feelings, intuition, and matters of the heart. Cup cards speak about relationships (familial, platonic, or romantic), love, compassion, emotional well-being, and the depth of your emotional experiences.

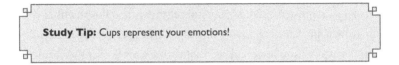

Study Tip: Cups represent your emotions!

Swords (Air)

The suit of Swords is associated with the element of air. Swords and air represent intellect, logic, thoughts, ideas, decision-making, mental health, and a sharp mind (swords are sharp).

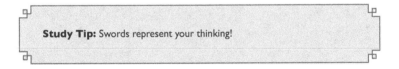

Study Tip: Swords represent your thinking!

Pentacles (Earth)

The suit of Pentacles is associated with the element of earth. Pentacles and earth represent the physical world, material possessions, practical matters, and my personal favorite, money (pentacles are coins!). These cards talk about your finances, career stability, physical well-being, and the practical application of skills and resources.

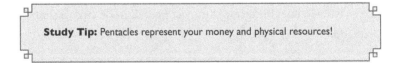

Study Tip: Pentacles represent your money and physical resources!

Understanding the Court Cards

Each suit consists of four court cards, which are the Page, Knight, Queen, and King. The court cards in tarot represent the people and energies of different individuals or "characters" that influence our lives and experiences. They are the royal families of each suit and bounce around a tarot reading adding flair and flamboyance.

Pages

The Pages represent childlike or youthful energy and the potential for growth and learning. They symbolize curiosity, new beginnings, and the exploration of new ideas. Pages bring a sense of enthusiasm and open-mindedness to situations while also bringing a hint of immaturity due to their youth. Pages are the tarot's fresh-faced newbies. They are like the interns of the court cards—ready to dive in headfirst with wide eyes and a touch of innocence.

> **Study Tip:** Think of the Page as the baby of the royal family! What would someone with the maturity of a child do in the situation?

Knights

The Knights represent action (with a pinch of recklessness), movement, and motivation. They symbolize the pursuit of goals and are the wild and adventurous souls of tarot. The Knight brings a sense of energy, passion, and enthusiasm to situations. They are like the action heroes of the court cards, always up for a thrilling quest or a daring voyage. The Knight carries adolescent energy and due to this, may sometimes bring immaturity or poor decision-making into a situation.

> **Study Tip:** Think of the Knight as an adolescent or teenager in the royal family! What would someone with the maturity of a teenager do in the situation?

Queens

The Queens represent mature feminine energy and nurturing qualities. They symbolize wisdom, compassion, and mastery over their suit and element. The Queens are powerful and exude confidence while ruling with grace. The Queen is so good at what she does that she now sits on the throne.

> **Study Tip:** Think of the Queen as the mother of the royal family! What would someone with the wisdom of a mother do in the situation?

Kings

The Kings in the court cards symbolize mature masculine energy and leadership. They symbolize authority, power, and mastery over their suit and element. They are like CEOs—the ones in charge and calling the shots.

> **Study Tip:** Think of the King as the father of the royal family! What would the King do to protect his kingdom?

Symbolism in the Tarot

Symbols in tarot play a crucial role in shaping the interpretation of each card and the messages they convey. Whether it is the in-your-face imagery of the Major Arcana or the more subtle symbolism of the Minor Arcana, every symbol has a story to tell and a lesson to teach. This list describes the most common symbols that can be found in tarot, and each symbol offers a unique perspective on the human experience and the eternal quest for meaning and purpose. By understanding the significance of these symbols, you will better notice helpful signposts along your spiritual journey and in the tarot deck itself.

A Hand Reaching Out
A hand reaching out symbolizes an offering, giving, or receiving.

A Sword Held Up
A sword held up signifies that a decision has not yet been made and suggests that the holder may still be in deliberation.

A Sword Held Down
A sword held down signifies that a decision has been made.

Armor
Armor represents protection, strength, and resilience.

Blindfold
A blindfold symbolizes indecision, hidden truths, and the need for introspection.

Bridge
A bridge represents connection or transition.

Castle
A castle is a symbol of strength, security, and achievement.

City/Town
A city or a town represents community, society, and civilization.

Clouds
Clouds are a symbol of uncertainty, lack of clarity, confusion, or hidden aspects.

Cliff
A cliff represents a need for careful navigation due to the risk of falling off.

Crops
Crops symbolize abundance, prosperity, and the fruitful results of hard work.

Crown
A crown is a symbol of authority, power, achievement, and earned respect.

Grapes
Grapes are a symbol of abundance, prosperity, and fertility.

Lake/Ocean/River
These bodies of water signify emotions, depth, and the unconscious.

Laurel Wreath
The laurel wreath is a symbol of victory, achievement, and honor.

Lemniscate
A lemniscate is often referred to as the infinity symbol and represents limitless possibilities and the interconnectedness of all things.

Mercurial Wings

Mercurial Wings represent the influence of the Roman messenger God, Mercury (or Hermes, in Greek mythology). It signifies swift communication, agility, business, and traveling.

Moon

The moon represents intuition, mystery, and the subconscious mind.

Mountains

Mountains represent challenges and obstacles in a journey, and the experiences you will have in overcoming them. Climbing the mountain is also the path to spiritual enlightenment.

Ouroboros

The Ouroboros, or the serpent eating its tail, is the symbol of the cyclical nature of all things, renewal, and eternity.

Red Feather

A red feather represents vitality, passion, and spiritual connection.

Red Rose

A red rose symbolizes love, desire, and passion.

Pomegranates

Pomegranates symbolize fertility and abundance due to their numerous seeds.

Scales
Scales are a symbol of balance, justice, and impartiality.

Ship
A ship is associated with journeys, adventures, movement, and incoming manifestations.

Snake
A snake represents knowledge, transformation, healing, and regeneration.

Sphinx
The sphinx represents mystery, riddles, and hidden knowledge.

Star
A star is a symbol of hope, guidance, and inspiration, and represents a connection to the cosmos.

Sun
The sun represents success, joy, optimism, and enlightenment.

Tora
Tora is Hebrew for "law" and represents wisdom, divine guidance, and spiritual teachings.

White Lily
A white lily is a symbol of purity and a connection to the divine.

Yod

The *Yod* is the tenth letter of the Hebrew alphabet and is a symbol of divine influence, guidance, and blessings.

Colors in the Tarot

Colors in tarot cards can add layers of meaning to your readings. They are not just there to make the cards look pretty; they are also packed with symbolism and can offer valuable insights into the energy and messages of each card. Whether it is a vibrant red's passionate intensity or a soothing blue's calm serenity, colors can evoke emotions, convey themes, and illuminate hidden truths within the cards.

Your homework is to pay close attention to the colors that appear on each card, as they are like secret clues. By understanding the significance of colors in tarot, you will unlock a new level of depth and understanding in your readings, allowing you to connect more deeply with the tarot.

Black

Black is associated with mystery and secrecy and represents transformation and the need to embrace the unknown with courage. It can symbolize the depths of the subconscious and the spiritual need to explore one's inner self. It may also signify unseen forces at play.

Blue

Blue is associated with intuition and can represent calmness, serenity, and connection to the divine. It can also signify the need for communication and self-expression and the pursuit of higher knowledge.

Green

Green represents growth and abundance as it is associated with the earth. It can represent the flourishing of opportunities and manifestations that are in progress.

Gray

Gray can represent indecision and indicate a need for neutrality and balance. It can suggest a need to avoid extremes while navigating situations with a composed and unbiased mindset.

Orange

Orange is the color of energy, creativity, and enthusiasm. It symbolizes passion, vitality, and the spark of inspiration that encourages the exploration of one's desires and personal goals.

Red

Red is associated with power, passion, action, and energy. It can also signify courage, strength, and the pursuit of goals with determination.

White

White represents purity, clarity, and spiritual enlightenment. It often symbolizes a blank slate, new beginnings, and the potential for spiritual growth, as well as divine guidance, truth, and the need to approach situations with honesty and integrity.

Yellow

Yellow is associated with optimism, joy, and intellect. Yellow can represent a period of learning, expanding one's awareness, and approaching challenges with a positive mindset.

Numerology in the Tarot

Numbers are more than just mathematical symbols; they are powerful signs that convey different meanings. From the limitless potential of the number zero to the culmination and completion represented by the number ten, each number in between carries its own unique vibration and energy. Each number offers valuable insights into the stages of a situation, progression of events, or aspects of life, adding additional information to your reading and helping you gain clarity and perspective.

Zero

Zero represents pure potential—or the absence thereof—of what has yet to be manifested. The Fool is the only card in the deck that is numbered zero.

Ace

Ace represents new beginnings and opportunities. It signifies taking the first steps of a journey, or the beginning of a situation or phase.

Two

Two represents balance, partnerships, and choices. It signifies union, decision-making, and the need to find equilibrium in different areas of life.

Three

Three represents creativity, self-expression, and expansion. It signifies embracing your unique talents, pursuing artistic endeavors, and exploring new possibilities.

Four

Four represents stability, structure, and practicality. It signifies the need for a solid foundation, organization, and hard work to manifest your goals.

Five

Five represents change, conflict, and the need for adaptability. It signifies embracing the unknown and being open to the flow of life's fluctuations.

Six

Six represents cooperation. It signifies the importance of family, relationships, and creating a harmonious environment.

Seven

Seven represents introspection and changing perspective. It signifies the quest for a deeper understanding of self through reflection.

Eight

Eight represents diligence, mastery, and action. It signifies moving steadily to achieve your goals and the rewards of hard work.

Nine

Nine represents fulfillment and achievement. It signifies the culmination of your efforts leading to personal accomplishments.

Ten

Ten represents the completion of a cycle. It signifies reaching a milestone, celebrating success, and being ready for the next phase, bringing you back to Ace.

Study Tip: The numbers represent where you are in a cycle and the different steps in a journey. A card with Ace is step one of a journey. A card with Two is step two. A card with Three is step three, and so on, until you reach Ten, which is the last step of a journey. Once you complete Ten in the journey, you must start a new journey beginning again at the Ace. Each number builds upon the lessons and experiences of the preceding ones, offering a progression of events in a situation or life stage.

Astrological Associations

Each card has a corresponding celestial body and zodiac sign. Understanding these astrological associations adds an additional layer of depth and nuance when interpreting the meaning of each tarot card. These associations influence the unique qualities of each card, which shapes the narrative of the overall reading. For people well-versed in astrology, astrological associations also assist with the memorization of each card.

CELESTIAL BODIES

Mercury

Mercury represents expression, intellect, and adaptability. Cards associated with Mercury also highlight resourceful thinking, quick wit, and the art of effective communication.

Venus

Venus symbolizes love, harmony, and beauty. Cards associated with Venus not only speak of relationships but also refer to the appreciation of beautiful things and aesthetics.

Earth

Earth represents grounding, stability, and the tangible aspects of life. Cards associated with Earth relate to practical matters, material concerns, and your connection to the physical world.

Mars

Mars represents energy and passion. Cards associated with Mars relate to control, power, and assertiveness, as well as the driving force that pushes you forward and encourages you to take action.

Jupiter

Jupiter is a symbol of growth and expansion. Cards associated with Jupiter represent abundance, luck, and new opportunities.

Saturn

Saturn represents structure, discipline, and responsibility. Cards associated with Saturn symbolize limitations, control, ambitious pursuits, and the potential rewards that come from achieving those pursuits.

Uranus

Uranus symbolizes innovation and rebellion. Cards associated with Uranus represent the spirit of forward-thinking, uniqueness, and the unpredictability that comes with trying to initiate new ideas.

Neptune

Neptune represents mysticism, enlightenment, and intuition. Cards associated with Neptune delve into the world of the dreamer and encourage you to explore the depths of intuition and spirituality.

Pluto

Pluto represents death, rebirth, and transformation. Cards associated with Pluto are related to regeneration and the resilience required to undergo profound change.

The Moon

The Moon represents intuition, dreams, and the ebb and flow of emotions. Cards associated with the Moon delve into the hidden aspects of life, revealing that which is hidden, and illuminating your inner world.

The Sun

The Sun is a symbol of vitality, illumination, and life force. Cards associated with the Sun embody success, positivity, and the clarity the comes with understanding and awareness.

ZODIAC SIGNS

Aries

Aries represents initiative, courage, and spontaneity. Cards associated with Aries reflect the intense, bold energy needed to pursue one's goals.

Taurus

Taurus symbolizes stability, determination, and stubbornness. Cards associated with Taurus represent material comfort and matters of the earthly realm.

Gemini
Gemini represents communication, adaptability, and intellectual agility. Cards associated with Gemini symbolize versatility and the ability to explore ideas from various perspectives.

Cancer
Cancer represents emotions, intuition, and receptivity. Cards associated with Cancer reflect themes involving feelings or the need to nurture aspects of self, family, or home.

Leo
Leo represents confidence, loyalty, and generosity. Cards associated with Leo symbolize passionate leadership and creative expression.

Virgo
Virgo symbolizes attention to detail, analysis, and practicality. Cards associated with Virgo embody the pursuit of perfection through a critical and reserved approach.

Libra
Libra represents balance, harmony, and partnerships. Cards associated with Libra embody themes concerning justice or the need for balance in relationships.

Scorpio
Scorpio represents intense transformation. Cards associated with Scorpio represent death and rebirth, regeneration, and the need for resilience.

Sagittarius
Sagittarius symbolizes exploration, optimism, and the pursuit of knowledge. Cards associated with Sagittarius represent the expansion

of the inner self through evolving thoughts and ideas or the expansion of the outer world through an increase of material resources.

Capricorn

Capricorn symbolizes structure, determination, and duty. Cards associated with Capricorn embody themes of accomplishing or failing at achieving your goals.

Aquarius

Aquarius represents innovation, humanitarianism, and rebellion. Cards associated with Aquarius embody themes of out-of-the-box thinking, independence, and progressiveness.

Pisces

Pisces symbolizes intuition, spiritual insight, and creativity. Cards associated with Pisces are related to the imagination and the fluidity of emotions.

CHAPTER 4

The Fool's Guide on How to Do a Tarot Reading

Understanding Your Role as the Tarot Reader

As a tarot reader, your mission, should you choose to accept it, is to help people—or yourself—tap into their inner wisdom, find their courage, and take charge of their destinies. It is essential to understand your role and responsibilities during a reading, and contrary to popular belief, you are not a fortune-teller or a mind reader. Instead, you play a crucial role in facilitating insight, guidance, and clarity. You are not here to predict the future or give people all the answers on a silver platter. That role is for fortune cookies. Instead, think of yourself as a spiritual detective, here to help them connect the dots in their lives.

Your role involves offering empathetic listening, compassionate guidance, and practical advice based on the insights gleaned from the cards. You have a responsibility to uphold ethical standards in your practice. This includes respecting client confidentiality, providing honest readings, and avoiding making predictions that could cause harm or distress. Above all, your role as a tarot reader is to empower those you read for to make informed decisions and take positive action in their lives. By offering insights, encouragement, and support, you help people tap into their inner wisdom and take control of their life and their destinies.

Getting Started

Choosing the Right Tarot Deck

Most books will tell you to pick a deck that you are energetically drawn to. That is not this book. If you want to learn and understand the fundamentals of tarot, use the Rider-Waite-Smith tarot deck.

CLEANSING AND CHARGING YOUR TAROT CARDS

Cleansing and charging your tarot cards are essential practices that help maintain their energy and keep them in tune with your intentions. Over time, your cards can pick up energy from various sources, including your emotions, the environments they are used in, and the people who handle them. Cleansing and charging them regularly helps reset their energy and ensure accurate readings. You would not want your cards dragging around negative vibes like a bad breakup, would you? Now, let us get those cards squeaky clean.

Smoke Cleansing

One of the most common methods for cleansing tarot cards is smoke cleansing. You can use sage, palo santo, or other cleansing herbs to pass the cards through the smoke, effectively clearing away any negative energy and leaving them feeling refreshed.

Crystal Cleansing

If crystals are more your style, you can place your tarot cards on a crystal cluster, such as clear quartz or selenite, overnight to absorb any unwanted energy and recharge them with positive vibrations.

Moonlight Cleansing

Harness the power of the moon by placing your tarot cards under the light of the full moon overnight. The moon's energy will cleanse and charge the cards, leaving them ready for use.

Salt Cleansing

You can also sprinkle a small amount of sea salt over your tarot cards or place them in a sealed bag with salt for twenty-four hours. The salt will absorb any negative energy, leaving your cards feeling purified and revitalized.

Intention Setting

Finally, you can cleanse and charge your tarot cards simply by setting your intention. Hold the cards in your hands and visualize them being surrounded by white light, cleansing away any impurities and infusing them with positive energy.

CREATING A SACRED SPACE FOR READINGS

Creating a sacred space for your tarot readings is essential for setting the right mood and energy. It is a space where you can connect with your higher knowing, spirit guides, and the energy of the cards without any distractions. Here are some steps to help you create your sacred space.

Choose a Sacred Space

Find a quiet and peaceful spot where you will not be disturbed during your readings. This could be a corner of your room, a cozy nook, or even a dedicated altar space.

Clear the Energy

Before you begin your readings, take a moment to clear the energy of the space. You can do this by smoke cleansing with sage, palo santo, or your preferred cleansing herb. Light the herb and waft the smoke around the room, focusing on the corners and areas where energy may feel stagnant.

Set the Mood

Create a soothing atmosphere by dimming the lights, lighting candles, or playing soft music in the background. You want to create an environment that feels calm and inviting.

Decorate Your Sacred Space

Personalize your sacred space with mystical items that are meaningful to you, such as crystals, sacred symbols, or spiritual artwork. These items can help enhance your connection to the divine and set the intention for your readings.

Use Sacred Tools

Keep your tarot cards, crystals, and any other divination tools you use in your sacred space. Treat them with respect, as they are powerful instruments for connecting with the spiritual realm.

Intention Setting

Before each reading, take a moment to set your intentions for the session. You can do this by silently stating your intention or saying a short prayer, asking for guidance and clarity.

Practice Grounding

Ground yourself before and after each reading to maintain a strong connection to the earth and to stay balanced. You can do this using a meditation technique by visualizing roots growing from your feet into the earth or by simply taking a few deep breaths and centering yourself.

Conducting a Tarot Reading

SHUFFLING AND CUTTING THE DECK
Shuffling and cutting the deck helps to infuse your energy into the cards. Here is how to shuffle and cut the deck.

Shuffling
People have a lot of questions about how to shuffle. "Should I use my left hand or my right?" "What if I can't keep the cards from clumping together?" Do not over think this one, just mix them up.

Intention Setting
As you shuffle the cards, focus on your intention for the reading. Whether you are seeking clarity, guidance, or insight into a specific question or situation, this will infuse your purpose into the cards.

Cutting the Deck
Hold the deck in your nondominant hand and use your dominant hand to split the deck into two or more piles. Some readers like to cut the deck once, while others prefer to cut it multiple times for added randomness. Cut the deck in a way that feels right for you.

Recombining the Deck
After cutting the deck, bring the piles back together into a single stack. Some readers like to perform a final shuffle at this stage to ensure that the cards are thoroughly mixed before beginning the reading. Again, do what feels right for you. Once the deck is shuffled and cut to your satisfaction, it is ready to be laid out for the reading.

READING THE CARDS

Once you have shuffled and cut the deck, draw cards and lay them out for your tarot reading. This process involves selecting the cards that will provide insight into the question or situation and arranging them in a spread that reflects the overall theme of your reading. Here is how to do it.

Intention Setting

Before drawing any cards, take a moment to focus your intention on the question or the area of life you want to explore. This helps to guide your subconscious mind and ensures that the cards you draw are aligned with your intention.

Drawing the Cards

There are several methods for drawing cards. You can draw a single card for a quick answer to a specific question, or you can draw multiple cards for a more comprehensive reading. As you draw each card, pay attention to any thoughts, feelings, or sensations that come up as these can add additional insights to a reading.

Laying Out the Spread

Once you have drawn your cards, it is time to lay them out in a spread (see Chapter 5). There are countless tarot spreads to choose from, ranging from simple three-card spreads to more complex layouts like the Celtic Cross. Pick a spread that resonates with the question and arrange the cards accordingly.

Interpreting the Cards

With your cards laid out before you, start by considering each card individually, paying attention to its symbolism, imagery, and meaning. Then, look at how the cards interact with each other within the spread, noting any patterns, contrasts, or connections between them. Finally, consider the overall theme or message of the reading as a whole.

Reflect and Integrate

Once you have completed the reading, take some time to reflect on the messages you have received and how they apply to the question or situation. Consider any action steps or changes that need to be made based on the insights gained from the reading.

As you continue the Fool's Journey of tarot, do not forget to nurture your practice and continue expanding your knowledge and skills. Whether you are reading for yourself, your friends and family, or clients, may your tarot practice bring you clarity, insight, and empowerment on this journey of self-discovery and spiritual growth.

CHAPTER 5

The Fool's Guide to Tarot Spreads

What Is a Tarot Spread?

Tarot spreads are like a roadmap for your tarot reading, guiding you through the twists and turns of the cards. A tarot spread is a specific arrangement of cards drawn during a reading. Each position in the arrangement has a designated meaning that helps to guide a tarot reader through a tailored narrative that is easier to interpret. Each position in a tarot spread addresses a specific aspect of a question or a situation. Think of it as a reading map that provides direction and structure to a reading instead of dealing with random cards laid down without order.

Choosing the Right Tarot Spread

For beginners, it is helpful to start with simple spreads, such as a one-card spread or a three-card spread. A Past-Present-Future spread is simple and provides an opportunity for gradual learning. Larger spreads like the Celtic Cross can be phased in as your comfort level grows and your understanding increases.

Using a Tarot Spread

Formulate a Clear Question

Before laying the cards, clearly phrase and articulate your question. The biggest issue people have with formulating questions is not being honest about what they want to know. The truth is, you picked up the cards with the intention of asking if the homeboy from two nights ago likes you, but instead ask, "Tarot, what does our future have in store?" Suddenly you are surprised when the cards give you a confusing answer. My dear Fool, that was not what you came here for. Ask the truth and make your truth clear and concise.

Do Not Reject Your Higher Self

A tarot spread provides structure, but your inner knowing given by your higher self is also capable of guiding you and your reading. Nurturing the relationship between structure and the spontaneous insights brought to you by your inner knowing will help to develop your intuition.

Honor the Card Positions

Respect the placement of each card, as each position in the arrangement carries a unique significance that adds to the overall narrative.

Weave a Story

Tarot is great for using as a storytelling tool. Use the pictures on each card in a tarot spread to weave together a story like those you used to read in picture books as a kid. This will help you piece together a reading.

One-Card Tarot Spreads

One-card tarot spreads focus on a particular energy that carries a specific message. Try practicing these one-card spreads in your daily one-card tarot readings.

The Snapshot Spread

This tarot spread can be used to provide a snapshot of the energy present in your question or situation.

METHOD

★ Shuffle the cards while focusing on your question or situation.

★ Draw one card.

★ Reflect on the card's symbolism and how it relates.

> **Study Tip:** Use this tarot spread in the morning to get a snapshot of the energy surrounding your day or in the evening to get a better understanding of what happened during the day.

The Affirmation Spread

This spread offers a daily affirmation aligning your energy with a positive intention.

METHOD

- ★ Shuffle the cards while thinking about the qualities that you wish to have or the traits you want to work on.

- ★ Draw one card.

- ★ Embrace the affirmation that the card represents or the lesson it is trying to teach you.

Three-Card Tarot Spreads

A three-card tarot spread is versatile and brings more depth to your readings without adding overwhelming complexity.

Past-Present-Future Spread

This is a classic spread that explores the energies in your journey by revealing the influences of the past, the current energies of the present, and the potential outcome in the future.

Card 1
Past

Card 2
Present

Card 3
Future

METHOD

* ★ Shuffle the cards while focusing on your situation.

* ★ Draw one card for the past, one card for the present, and one card for the future.

* ★ Reflect.

Mind-Heart-Soul Spread

This spread explores what is on your mind, in your heart, and the inner knowing from your higher self. This spread will help you assess if you are in alignment with your true self.

Card 1
Mind

Card 2
Heart

Card 3
Soul

METHOD

* ★ Shuffle the cards while focusing on your situation.

* ★ Draw one card for the mind, one for the heart, and one for the soul.

* ★ Reflect.

You-Me-Us Spread

This spread explores the dynamics within a relationship and the feelings and perspectives of the individuals involved. It can be used for romantic relationships and friendships and to gain insights into the connections of those at work and in families.

Card 1
You (Them) or Person A

Card 2
Me or Person B

Card 3
Us

METHOD

★ Shuffle the cards while focusing on the relationship or connection.

★ Draw one card for Person A, one card for Person B, and one card for the relationship dynamics.

★ Reflect.

Celtic Cross Tarot Spread

In the world of tarot, the Celtic Cross spread is the headliner. It is a classic and arguably one of the most used spreads by tarot readers. This ten-card spread is thorough and can offer deep insights into any situation.

Card 1: Significator

This card represents the querent (the person asking the question), current situation, or the central issue. It lays the foundation for the entire spread.

Card 2: Challenges (Crossing Energies)

This card represents the challenges or crossing energies impacting the situation.

Card 3: Consciousness
This card represents other influences impacting the situation that you are aware of.

Card 4: Subconsciousness
This card represents other influences impacting the situation that you are *not* aware of.

Card 5: Past
This card represents past events impacting the current situation.

Card 6: Future
This card represents the influences impacting the situation that will occur in the future.

Card 7: Attitude
This card represents your attitudes and beliefs regarding the situation.

Card 8: Environment
This card represents the external influences or people impacting the situation.

Card 9: Hopes, Dreams, and Fears
This card represents your hopes and fears regarding the outcome of the situation.

Card 10: Final Outcome
This card represents how the situation will resolve itself.

Part 2

The Fool's Guide to the Major Arcana

CHAPTER 6

The Major Arcana

0. The Fool

A FRESH START

Astrological Associations

Celestial Body
Uranus

Zodiac Sign
Aquarius

Keywords

New beginnings, leap of faith, potential, innocence, spontaneity, taking calculated risks.

Understanding the Fool

The Fool, the star of the tarot show, is depicted as a young, carefree man carrying a small knapsack full of worldly possessions and tools that he is bringing with him from his past life on his new adventure. He is standing on the edge of a rocky cliff with no visible safety net requiring him to take a leap of faith. Behind him is his guard dog and spirit companion guiding him into this new phase of his journey of life. The mountains represent the potential for achievement and success. The flower represents the Fool's childlike innocence and purity as his carefree nature has caused him to stop to smell the roses as he walks up to the edge of the cliff. Although the Fool is not carrying a map to tell him where he is going, the sun is illuminating the way guiding him on his new path.

Card Meaning

You are the Fool! People oftentimes view the musings of tarot to be talking about some far out elusive spiritual concept. I am here to burst that bubble. This card represents you (the person asking the question), the Fool, embarking on something new in life.

The Fool is the only card in the deck without a number. Its zero forms a complete circle and signifies the untapped potential at the beginning of a journey. The Fool teaches you to take a leap of faith and trust in yourself as you begin a new cycle, seek new opportunities, and navigate new experiences, phases, and possible challenges.

Notice the Fool has a tiny bag and is not carrying luggage. It is okay to leave things, people, and baggage behind. Take only the things that serve your highest good and are meant for your greatest potential into your new phase of life. As the Fool, you must learn to let go of fear and take risks. Being too comfortable in your routine and familiar surroundings can make you become stagnant and hinder your growth. When was the last time you allowed your courage and optimism to try something new to overrule your fear of failure? It is time for you to be the Fool and take that leap of faith.

> **Study Tip:** Notice that now he has both shoes on as he will have lost part of a shoe later in his journey (see Seven of Wands).

Affirmation

I embrace the journey of life with a curious spirit to allow for infinite possibilities.

Journal Prompts

★ What is a new beginning in your life that you are currently experiencing or anticipating? What excites you about this new beginning?

★ What is an expectation of a situation or person that you are holding onto? How would letting go of this expectation free you?

★ When was the last time you could be your authentic self? How can you incorporate more authenticity into your life?

I. The Magician

THE MASTER OF MANIFESTATION

Astrological Associations

Celestial Body
Mercury

Zodiac Sign
Gemini

Keywords
Manifestation, willpower, talent, creation, resourcefulness.

Understanding the Magician

The Magician wears a vibrant red robe and stands with a lemniscate (infinity symbol) above his head, which represents eternal potential and infinite possibilities. He is in a garden of red roses and white lilies and wields a wand pointed toward the sky (as above), channeling divine energy, while pointing his other finger toward the ground (so below), symbolizing the manifestation of this energy into his physical reality. On the table in front of him lies a wand, cup, sword, and pentacle, signifying the four suits of tarot and the tools that are at his disposal. His red robe represents passionate action, which increases the power he wields, and his white snake belt symbolizes his spiritual purity and the wisdom he holds.

Card Meaning

The Magician represents manifestation and the power of the mind to create reality. It symbolizes limitless potential and is a reminder that the tools needed to transform the world around you are at your disposal. The Magician empowers you to trust your ability to manifest your desires through focused intention and resourcefulness.

The Magician teaches you that your thoughts shape your reality. You are the magician in your life and can harness the resources available to you to begin cultivating the reality that you wish to experience. Manifestation requires conscious creation. The Magician is you, the Fool, and who you have become after you took your leap of faith.

Bibbidi, Bobbidi, Boo!

Affirmation

I possess all the tools of creation: the wand of intention, the cup of emotion, the sword of intellect, and the pentacle of manifestation.

Journal Prompts

★ What are your unique skills and talents that you bring to
   the table? How could you use them to move closer to your
   dream reality?

★ What is a goal that you have? What actions, mindset, or
   resources do you need to bring that goal to fruition? What are
   some steps you could take today to begin manifesting that goal?

★ If you could wield a magic wand and change one aspect of your
   life right now, what would it be? What are some steps you could
   take today to begin manifesting that change?

II. The High Priestess

THE KEEPER OF SECRETS

Astrological Associations

Celestial Body
Moon

Zodiac Sign
Cancer

Keywords
Intuition, subconscious, mysticism, divine feminine, inner wisdom.

Understanding the High Priestess

The High Priestess, wearing a blue robe symbolizing intuition, serenity, and a connection to the divine, sits on a throne. She wears a moon crown representing her authority over intuition and the depths of the mind, and holds the sacred scroll of Torah, Hebrew for "divine law," in her lap. The cross on her chest represents the balance between the four elements: fire, water, air, and earth. Beneath her feet, her flowing robe mirrors the fluidity of water, a visual representation of her connection to her intuition. At her feet rests a crescent moon, a symbol of her connection to the cyclical nature of the moon phases as a divine feminine. She sits positioned between two pillars, the black pillar marked "B" and the white pillar marked "J," representing Boaz and Jachin from the Temple of Solomon. These pillars signify the duality between light and dark and the conscious and subconscious that the High Priestess moves effortlessly between. Behind her is a veil, which signifies the hidden knowledge she guards, and it is adorned with pomegranates, symbolizing life, fertility, and abundance.

Card Meaning

The High Priestess represents trusting your intuition and being open to receiving guidance from the spiritual world. It symbolizes taking a step back from the outer world to look inward at your subconscious, as the answer is right below the surface. This card signifies a time of introspection as you reflect on your inner wisdom.

The High Priestess teaches you to look inward when searching for the answer. In a world full of noise, sometimes the best thing you can do is sit in silence. Listen to your inner voice as it is full of knowledge. There is a lot of information that resides in the stillness.

Affirmation

I trust my intuition and allow it to guide me on my journey.

Journal Prompts

★   Reflect on a recent situation where your intuition guided you.
    What did you learn from that experience?

★   Reflect on a dream that you had recently. Identify any
    prominent symbols within it. Use your intuition to decipher
    these symbols to decode the messages they might hold for you.

★   Imagine that you stepped through the veil behind the High
    Priestess. What mysteries would you want to uncover in the
    depths of your subconscious? What parts of yourself do you
    want to explore and understand better?

III. The Empress

THE MOTHER

Astrological Associations

Celestial Body
Venus

Zodiac Sign
Taurus

Keywords
Fertility, creation, abundance, motherhood.

Understanding the Empress

The Empress depicts a woman wearing a crown adorned with twelve stars, symbolizing the twelve signs of the zodiac, its guiding influence, and her profound link to the universe. Seated on her throne, she wears a dress adorned with pomegranates, their seeds symbolizing life and fertility. Her scepter, topped with a globe, signifies her dominion over the physical realm, enabling her to manifest abundance in the material world. She sits in a forest representing abundance and is surrounded by a wheat field, a testament to the bountiful harvest that she cultivates. At her feet lies a shield with the symbol of Venus, a sign of femininity, love, and the beauty of the creations she brings into existence.

Card Meaning

The Empress represents a period of creating or receiving abundance, which can come in the form of material wealth, fertility, or emotional fulfillment. This card symbolizes embracing your nurturing side as this cultivates a creative and supportive environment that is helpful for calling in abundance.

The Empress teaches you about the importance of nurturing and caring for yourself. Often, people focus on caring for others resulting in them denying their own needs. To properly embrace abundance, it is wise to ensure that your giving and receiving are in balance.

Affirmation

I am a creator of life and beauty, bringing forth love and abundance into the world.

Journal Prompts

★　Contemplate your abundance in your life. In what areas do you feel abundant? If you do not feel abundant, where could you enhance the flow of abundance?

★   In what ways do you care for yourself? Do you honor your
    wants and desires? Are there areas in life where you could
    improve in providing more support and compassion
    to yourself?

★   Think about the influence of maternal figures in your life. How
    have they shaped your understanding of nurturing and care?
    What lessons have you learned from these relationships? Are
    there any lessons you could unlearn?

IV. The Emperor

THE FATHER

Astrological Associations

Celestial Body
Mars

Zodiac Sign
Aries

Keywords
Authority, leadership, power, structure, stability, fatherhood.

Understanding the Emperor

The Emperor depicts a man wearing a crown that symbolizes his authority. He sits on a stone throne adorned with ram heads. The sturdiness of the stone represents stability and structure, which complements the assertive and initiating nature associated with Aries. He wears red robes over a suit of armor, with the red robes signifying both passion and strength and the protective armor emphasizing the need for resilience in leadership. The scepter he holds symbolizes his dominion over his worldly realm. There are mountains behind him, which represent challenges and obstacles, and he sits in front of them, signifying that he has overcome those challenges.

Card Meaning

The Emperor represents leadership, power, and structure. It symbolizes the establishment of order needed to achieve your goals. The Emperor signifies that you are in control of your life and circumstances.

The Emperor teaches a need for structure and discipline to achieve your goals. To shape your reality requires that you use your personal authority. Embrace the responsibility that comes with establishing order to attain success in your life.

Affirmation

I am a sovereign being and embody strength, power, and authority in all areas of my life.

Journal Prompts

★ Where in your life could you benefit from more discipline? How could incorporating the qualities of the Emperor positively impact your life?

★ Reflect on the balance between structure and flexibility. Are
   there areas in your life where you could loosen control to bring
   about more balance?

★ Imagine yourself sitting on the Emperor's throne. What
   decisions would you make to improve the stability in your life?

V. The Hierophant

THE POPE

Astrological Associations

Celestial Body
Venus

Zodiac Sign
Taurus

Keywords
Tradition, institution, spiritual wisdom, marriage, teacher.

Understanding the Hierophant

The Hierophant depicts a religious leader, such as a pope, wearing ceremonial robes representing spiritual tradition and established practices and a crown with three nails at the top symbolizing the crucifixion of Jesus. He holds a staff with a papal cross (triple cross), which is the emblem of the Pope, in one hand and raises his other hand with two fingers, signifying a blessing. He sits between two pillars, representing duality and the ability to navigate between heaven and hell. Two men looking for guidance kneel at his feet, and a pair of keys signifying the answer to spiritual enlightenment rests on the ground.

Card Meaning

The Hierophant represents tradition and an established institution. It can signify a spiritual leader or mentor who holds spiritual knowledge for those seeking guidance and answers.

The Hierophant teaches you to explore the balance between tradition and the freedom you need for your personal spiritual growth. Tradition provides a framework that is helpful for leaning on, but it is important to examine whether it is beneficial to continue to conform or if it is time for you to create your unique path.

Affirmation

I find strength and comfort in following a path that aligns with my values and beliefs.

Journal Prompts

★   Reflect on a time when you followed a traditional path. What wisdom did you gain from this experience?

★   Are there areas in your life where you conform to people or systems? How does it impact your decision-making? Where would breaking away from these people or systems serve your higher purpose?

★   Reflect on your spiritual journey. Have you been drawn to any spiritual teachings or rituals? How have they influenced your beliefs and actions?

VI. The Lovers

CHOICE AND COMMITMENT

Astrological Associations

Celestial Body
Mercury

Zodiac Sign
Gemini

Keywords
Love, union, partnership, duality, choice.

Understanding the Lovers

The Lovers depicts Adam and Eve in the Garden of Eden, standing beneath the archangel Raphael, who represents healing, guidance, and divine influence. Their nakedness symbolizes purity, transparency, authenticity, and vulnerability. Eve stands in front of an apple tree that signifies temptation and desire and is being lured by a serpent that represents knowledge, choices, and the potential consequences that come with it. Adam stands in front of a tree of flames, symbolizing the burning bush and the presence of the Divine.

Card Meaning

The Lovers represents choices related to romantic connections, partnerships, friendships, and internal dilemmas. Represented by the sign of Gemini, it signifies the influence between duality and opposites and how that can affect your decision-making in these areas of life.

The Lovers teaches you to align your choices with your most authentic self by honoring your inner truth. This alignment will promote a sense of balance and harmony in your decision-making, as well as in how you experience the relationships in your life.

Affirmation

I am deserving of a deep and passionate love that uplifts and inspires me.

Journal Prompts

★ Reflect on a time when you felt torn between listening to your mind and following your heart. Did you ultimately choose your mind or your heart? Did this choice lead to your intended outcome?

★ Reflect on the idea of soulmates. Do you believe in the concept of soul connections, and if so, what qualities do you associate with soulmate relationships?

★   Imagine your ideal romantic relationship. What values, beliefs,
    and experiences exist in this relationship? What work can
    you do on yourself to work toward manifesting that vision in
    your life?

VII. The Chariot

THE PATH TO VICTORY

Astrological Associations

Celestial Body
Moon

Zodiac Sign
Cancer

Keywords
Forward movement, willpower, determination, focus, victory.

Understanding the Chariot

The Chariot depicts an armored warrior riding a chariot, symbolizing his control, willpower, and triumph over adversity. He wears a crown adorned with the sun, signifying success, and a laurel wreath, affirming victory. With a wand in hand, he demonstrates authority and control over his destiny. The black and white sphinxes represent opposing forces, while the absence of reins highlights his ability to balance and control them. The starry canopy above symbolizes divine guidance, guiding him on his Fool's Journey.

Card Meaning

The Chariot represents forward movement after overcoming obstacles and is a symbol of success and victory. It signifies that with determination, you have the strength to accomplish your goals if you stay focused and take decisive action to move forward in your life.

The Chariot teaches you to harness your willpower and drive to take control of your life and its circumstances as it is up to you to decide whether to move forward from difficult situations. Forward movement is propelled by a strong sense of purpose and progress is powered by perseverance.

Affirmation

I will harness my willpower and focus it toward achieving my goals and aspirations.

Journal Prompts

★ Reflect on areas of your life where you feel stuck. How can you tap into your inner strength and willpower to generate momentum to create positive change?

★ Where do you see areas of imbalance or opposing forces in your life? What has stopped you from restoring its equilibrium?

★   Imagine yourself riding the Chariot, confidently leading the
     way toward your desired destination. What sights do you see
     along this Fool's Journey? How do you navigate any challenges
     that arise with grace and determination?

VIII. Strength

TAMING THE INNER BEAST

Astrological Associations

Celestial Body
Sun

Zodiac Sign
Leo

Keywords
Resilience, inner strength, courage, compassion.

Understanding Strength

The Strength card depicts a woman calmly taming a lion, symbolizing inner strength, courage, and resilience. She uses a gentle touch as she grasps the lion's mouth to control its roar, symbolizing compassion and patience. The lemniscate (infinity symbol) above her head represents infinite potential and the cyclical nature of life's challenges, while the mountains in the background symbolize external obstacles that must be overcome. The woman's white robe symbolizes purity and spiritual enlightenment.

Card Meaning

Strength represents a need for you to find your inner strength through exercising resilience and courage and urges you to face your situation with composure. It symbolizes approaching situations with grace and having faith in your ability to approach challenges with a calm and centered mindset.

Strength teaches you that true power does not come from acts of aggression or dominance; it comes from compassion and self-control. Be patient with yourself when learning how to tame your inner beast, as true power lies in your grace.

Affirmation

I am strong, resilient, and capable of conquering any obstacle that comes my way.

Journal Prompts

★ Think about areas of your life that require the use of more inner strength. What can you do to cultivate greater resilience and courage in those areas?

★ How would showing yourself greater compassion contribute to your sense of inner strength?

★   What does the lion on the Strength card represent to you? What
     aspects of your personality does it reflect?

IX. The Hermit

THE ROAD TO SELF-DISCOVERY

Astrological Associations

Celestial Body
Mercury

Zodiac Sign
Virgo

Keywords
Introspection, solitude, enlightenment, inner guidance.

Understanding the Hermit

The Hermit depicts a man standing on the edge of a mountain with a lantern in hand. The lantern is illuminated by a star, representing his inner light and the pursuit of his personal truth. The mountain represents the spiritual journey and the challenges one must overcome to reach enlightenment. His isolation symbolizes a time of introspection and withdrawal from the external world to seek inner wisdom. He leans on a staff, signifying support and guidance on his Fool's Journey.

Card Meaning

The Hermit represents a time of introspection and seeking solitude to find guidance from within. The Hermit symbolizes trusting your intuition and listening to the voice of your higher self.

The Hermit teaches you to listen to your inner voice as this is where your truth comes from. The world can be a noisy place, but not everything you hear is in alignment with your personal journey.

AFFIRMATION
I embrace solitude as an opportunity for self-discovery and enlightenment.

JOURNAL PROMPTS

★ Reflect on a recent experience that brought you into a place of solitude. What realizations about this situation did you gain during this time of introspection?

★ Explore your idea of enlightenment and spiritual growth. What steps can you take to deepen your connection with your higher self to cultivate your inner wisdom?

★   Think about a time when you trusted your intuition and it
    led you in the right direction. What can you do to continue
    building trust in your intuitive ability?

X. Wheel of Fortune

FATE VS. DESTINY

*"There is a difference between fate and destiny.
Fate happens to you. Destiny is decided by you."*

—Mystic Rainn

Astrological Associations

Celestial Body

Jupiter

Zodiac Signs
Taurus, Leo, Scorpio, Aquarius

Keywords
Destiny, luck, opportunity, change.

Understanding the Wheel of Fortune
The Wheel of Fortune depicts a large wheel surrounded by four
winged creatures representing the four fixed signs of the zodiac:
the lion (Leo), the bull (Taurus), the eagle (Scorpio), and the angel
(Aquarius). At the top of the wheel sits the Sphinx holding a sword,
representing wisdom and the mysteries of the universe. On the left of
the wheel is a snake representing transformation and regeneration. On
the right of the wheel is Anubis, the jackal-headed ancient Egyptian
god of the afterlife, death, and rebirth. On the wheel is written "Tora,"
which is Hebrew for "divine law" and represents divine guidance
and spiritual teachings. The wheel symbolizes the cycles of life, fate,
and destiny.

Card Meaning
The Wheel of Fortune represents a time of change that is brought
to you by a stroke of luck or a new opportunity. It symbolizes the
cyclical nature of life as the wheel is always turning, and as it turns, it
brings changes.

But here is the thing about luck—it is neutral. It is neither good nor
bad until it is assigned a meaning by you. The way the wheel turns is
determined by your perspective of life and current situations, but most
importantly, your sheer amount of arrogant will and audacity to move
forward in the direction you want.

So, my dear Fool, which way will you choose?

Affirmation

I accept abundance, success, and opportunity in my life as the Wheel of Fortune turns in my favor.

Journal Prompts

★   Explore your ideas of fate and destiny. Have you been automatically surrendering to what fate brings you? How can you empower yourself to write a more heroic story to shape your destiny?

★   Think about a recent stroke of luck or unexpected opportunity that came your way. How did you respond to it? Were you open to receiving it? If not, what could you do to keep your energy field open to receiving unexpected opportunities in the future?

★   Write about a time when you felt a sense of synchronicity or alignment with the universe. What were the signs you received?

XI. Justice

WHAT GOES AROUND COMES AROUND

Astrological Associations

Celestial Body
Venus

Zodiac Sign
Libra

Keywords
Fairness, balance, truth, accountability, karma.

Understanding Justice

Justice depicts a woman seated on a throne between two pillars, representing the balance between opposing forces, such as right and wrong. In one hand, she holds the sword of truth upright, symbolizing discernment and the ability to cut through illusions, and in the other hand, a set of scales signifying the need to weigh decisions carefully prior to making a decision. The throne symbolizes her authority, wisdom, and integrity.

Card Meaning

The Justice card represents fairness, balance, and accountability. It symbolizes that all actions and choices have consequences, and that the truth will prevail.

Justice teaches you that you are of the universe and the universe is of you. Karma does not happen to you; it is a reflection of you. You reap what you sow, so be mindful of your actions, for karma has no menu. You get served what you deserve.

Affirmation

I trust in the balance of the universe to guide me toward truth and justice.

Journal Prompts

★ Consider how you can incorporate the principles of fairness, balance, and integrity into your daily life. How can you work to be a more just and equitable person in your interactions with other people?

★ Reflect on the idea of karma and that your actions have both positive and negative consequences. Have you experienced any instances in your life where you felt that your karma played a role in the outcome of a situation?

★   Think about the role of forgiveness in the pursuit of justice.
    Is there someone in your life that you need to forgive to find
    closure and move forward?

XII. The Hanged Man

RENEWED PERSPECTIVE

Astrological Associations

Celestial Body
Neptune

Zodiac Sign
Pisces

Keywords
Perspective, pause, surrender, enlightenment.

Understanding the Hanged Man

The Hanged Man depicts a man suspended upside down from a tree.
His legs form the shape of the number four, symbolizing finding
stability and setting a foundation even while hanging upside down.
His hands are tied behind his back, representing surrender and
letting go of control. He has a calm expression, signifying a peaceful
acceptance of his circumstances, and his halo symbolizes his newfound
enlightenment gained from his surrender.

Card Meaning

The Hanged Man represents a change of perspective that is often
triggered by being in limbo or in a period of waiting. This card also
symbolizes feeling stuck in a certain situation.

The Hanged Man teaches you to let go of your attachments to
perceived outcomes and to embrace the present moment. By
surrendering, you step to the side and out of the way of what is truly
meant for you, and you open yourself to receive new perspectives and
a deeper understanding of life's circumstances.

Affirmation

*I trust that the universe has a higher plan for me, even if I cannot see it
at this moment.*

Journal Prompts

★ Consider the concept of surrender in your daily life. Are there
any areas where you struggle to let go and trust in the unfolding
of life? What steps can you take to surrender in those areas?

★ Think of a recent challenge or obstacle you faced. How would
adopting a different perspective change your experience or
approach to the situation?

★ Contemplate the role of patience in your life. Can you embrace periods of waiting and uncertainty, or do you struggle with impatience? How can you practice patience and trust in divine timing?

XIII. Death

REBIRTH

Astrological Associations

Celestial Body
Pluto

Zodiac Sign
Scorpio

Keywords
Transformation, transition, endings, change, resurrection.

Understanding Death

Death depicts the Grim Reaper atop a white horse. The Grim Reaper holds a black flag adorned with a white rose, a sharp contrast symbolizing purity in the darkness. Before him are people from various walks of life, including a King and a Bishop, illustrating that death respects no status or spiritual position. Two children kneel before him, which is a reminder that mortality spares no one, regardless of age or innocence. The ship in the background signifies the journey to the afterlife, while the rising sun on the horizon signifies the dawn of new beginnings.

Card Meaning

Death represents the end of a significant phase or cycle of your life, which is needed to make space for something new. It symbolizes transition and an upcoming renewal or rebirth.

Dun dun duuun! (cue dramatic sound effect)

Death is one of those cards that always adds a little pizzazz to a reading. My sense of humor makes it amusing for me to witness the reactions when this card emerges from the deck. Understandable, of course, as people often fear what they do not understand. Luckily for you, this Death is not about a physical demise; it is about transformation and growth, as any change brought by Death, even if painful, will always lead to your evolution as a spiritual being.

Affirmation

I embrace the cycle of life and death, knowing that endings pave the way for new beginnings.

Journal Prompts

★ Think about a recent time of change or transition in your life. How did you initially react to it? Were you excited? What about scared? What did you learn from the experience?

★ Consider a situation or an aspect of your life that you feel ready to release or let go of. What emotions arise when you imagine releasing it? How might you approach this process with courage and openness?

★ Imagine yourself as the figure of Death in the Tarot card, riding confidently into the unknown. What new opportunities do you envision on the horizon?

XIV. Temperance

BALANCE AND HARMONY

Astrological Associations

Celestial Body
Jupiter

Zodiac Sign
Sagittarius

Keywords
Balance, moderation, integration, healing.

Understanding Temperance

Temperance depicts an angel pouring water from one cup to another, symbolizing the alchemical process of transformation and the harmonious blending of the elements. With one foot on land and the other in water, the angel represents the balance between the emotional and physical realms, encouraging equilibrium in all aspects of life. The presence of the mountain signifies the challenges one must face and overcome to achieve inner harmony and balance. The rising sun represents the enlightenment and spiritual growth that come from successfully navigating these challenges.

Card Meaning

Temperance represents finding balance and moderation in your emotions, relationships, and actions. This card symbolizes finding a more stable approach to life and its circumstances.

Temperance teaches you the practice of moderation and self-control as you embark on the Fool's Journey. You are the creator of your reality and can steer your ship toward your ideal version of inner peace and balance.

Affirmation

I embrace balance and harmony in all aspects of my life.

Journal Prompts

★ In what areas of your life do you swing between extremes? How can you find a middle ground and create a more balanced approach?

★ Explore the concept of moderation in your consumption habits, whether it is related to food, technology, or other areas of your life. How can you practice mindful consumption and avoid excess?

★　Reflect on the concept of yin and yang and the balance between masculine and feminine energies within yourself. Are there any areas where you feel out of balance with these energies? How can you regain a sense of equilibrium?

XV. The Devil

YOU ARE YOUR OWN WORST ENEMY

Astrological Associations

Celestial Body
Saturn

Zodiac Sign
Capricorn

Keywords
Temptation, addiction, self-sabotage, bondage, shadow.

Understanding the Devil

The Devil depicts Baphomet, a horned-goat figure representing illusions, temptations, and desires. Adam and Eve from the Garden of Eden in the Lovers, are now bound to a pedestal, symbolizing their entrapment in the material world. The loosely hanging chains around their necks signify their potential to break free by seeing through the illusions. The torch held by the Devil represents the light of truth that shines through darkness and shadows, and the inverted pentagram on Baphomet's forehead symbolizes the corruption of spiritual energy and higher principles for selfish gains.

Card Meaning

The Devil is the shadow side of human nature and represents temptation and addictions. It symbolizes being caught in a web of self-imposed limitations that hold you back from being *you*. The Devil teaches you to confront your deepest fears, desires, and attachments, as they are the chains that hold you back from living as your authentic self.

This is the card that freaks out churchgoers and spooks the average tarot beginner. How ironic is it that those people are simply afraid of themselves? It is *you*, my dear Fool, who serves as your own Devil.

Affirmation

I release the chains of my negative patterns and behavior.

Journal Prompts

★ Think about areas of your life where you lie to yourself or deny your true desires. What is preventing you from being honest with yourself?

★ Consider the role of fear in your life. What fears or insecurities hold you back from pursuing your goals or living authentically?

How do these fears contribute to feelings of bondage or limitation?

★ Think about how addictions manifest in your life. This can include substance addiction, behavioral or emotional patterns, or unproductive thoughts that you find difficult to break free from. How do these addictions impact your sense of freedom and well-being?

XVI. The Tower

THE DESTROYER

Astrological Associations

Celestial Body
Mars

Zodiac Sign
Aries

Keywords
Upheaval, chaos, sudden change, destruction, liberation.

Understanding the Tower

The Tower depicts a tall tower engulfed in flames and being struck by lightning, with people jumping out of the windows. *Yods* rain down from the sky, representing divine intervention. The tower symbolizes the dismantling of old structures, beliefs, and systems, with the lightning signifying sudden change. The flames represent destruction and the purifying power of fire, and the people jumping symbolize the shedding of ego and the false self. The crown signifies worldly success and that even past achievements cannot stop this divine process.

Card Meaning

The Tower represents a sudden and profound change that may initially feel destructive or chaotic. It symbolizes the collapse of illusions, false beliefs, and outdated structures in your life.

In addition to the Devil, the Tower is one of the most feared cards in the tarot deck (I am not fond of it), but it teaches you that while change can be daunting, on the other side of it is liberation and renewal. After the Tower crumbles, you are left with a new foundation to build on. Sometimes, breakdowns are necessary to experience breakthroughs.

Affirmation

I am protected during times of upheaval and change.

Journal Prompts

★ What are your feelings about change or perceived upheaval? Are you resistant to it? Do you embrace it as an opportunity for growth and transformation?

★ Imagine yourself standing at the top of the Tower, witnessing its destruction. What illusions or false beliefs are being shattered? What new insights or revelations are emerging?

★ Write a letter to yourself from the perspective of the Tower,
   offering guidance and wisdom on navigating periods of
   upheaval and transformation in your life.

XVII. The Star

A BEACON OF HOPE

Astrological Associations

Celestial Body
Uranus

Zodiac Sign
Aquarius

Keywords
Hope, renewal, divine guidance, inspiration.

Understanding the Star

The Star depicts a naked woman pouring water from two pitchers. One into a pool and one onto the land. The pouring of water into the pool represents the flow of spiritual energy, and the pouring of water onto land symbolizes her renewing the earth around her contributing to the lush greenery. Her nakedness signifies vulnerability and authenticity. The eight-pointed star above her radiates light, representing hope, guidance, and divine intervention, and the seven smaller stars symbolize the seven chakras.

Card Meaning

The Star card represents maintaining hope and faith, even during times of uncertainty and adversity. It is the card of divine guidance and spiritual renewal.

The Star teaches you to remain open and receiving during tough times as hope acts as the glimmer of light in a sea of darkness. Keep your eyes set on the horizon because the sun will always rise again.

Affirmation

I understand that I must give space for my journey to unfold and know that I am supported every step of the way.

Journal Prompts

★ Think about a time when you felt discouraged. How did you find hope and resilience within yourself? What practices help you find hope and optimism even in the face of adversity?

★ Imagine yourself as a guiding light for others, radiating hope and inspiration to those around you. How can you share your wisdom and positivity with the world? What actions can you take to uplift and support others on their journey toward healing and renewal?

★ Reflect on the concept of divine timing in the universe's plan for you. Is there a situation in your life where you feel impatient or anxious about the outcome? How can you surrender to the flow of life and trust that everything is unfolding as it should?

XVIII. The Moon

THINGS ARE NOT WHAT THEY SEEM

Astrological Associations

Celestial Body
Neptune

Zodiac Sign
Pisces

Keywords
Mystery, hidden information, illusion, dreams, uncertainty.

Understanding the Moon

The Moon depicts a moonlit night sky with a full moon shining down upon a winding path. The full moon represents your intuition, and the winding path is lit by the moon's falling *yods*, symbolizing the divine guidance and illumination received on your journey of life, as well as the twists and turns you encounter along the way. The path winds between two pillars, symbolizing duality, and the balance between the conscious and unconscious realms. A domesticated dog and a wolf, signifying our tame and wild instincts, howl at the moon, while a crayfish emerges from the water, representing coming up from the depths of the unconscious mind.

Card Meaning

The Moon represents the unknown and signifies that illusions, fears, or uncertainty may be clouding your judgement or the situation. It also symbolizes the subconscious mind and everything that resides in it, such as your intuition or dreams.

The Moon teaches you that sometimes, things are not always what they seem and encourages you to use your intuition to guide you as you navigate through the mystery of your circumstances. Your inner guidance is your friend, as it will help you uncover the hidden truths.

My dear Fool, if questions about trust or deception are asked, let us hope this card does not make an appearance.

Affirmation

I seek to see through illusions.

Journal Prompts

★   Reflect on a recent dream you had. What symbols or messages stood out to you? What was it trying to tell you?

★   Think about the cycles and rhythms of your life. Are there any
     patterns or recurring themes that you notice?

★   Imagine yourself standing at a crossroads, with multiple paths
     stretching out before you. What fears or uncertainties come up
     as you think about each option? How would you determine the
     right path?

XIX. The Sun

EMBRACE YOUR BRILLIANCE

Astrological Associations

Celestial Body
Sun

Zodiac Sign
Leo

Keywords
Success, opportunities, abundance, confidence, self-esteem.

Understanding the Sun

The Sun card depicts a radiant sun, representing life force and enlightenment, shining brightly in a clear sky that symbolizes clarity, optimism, and boundless potential. A child rides a white horse, signifying innocence, purity, and the happiness that comes from embracing the present moment. The child holds a red flag, representing triumph over adversity. Surrounding them are vibrant sunflowers, symbolizing growth and the blossoming of possibilities. Behind the child and horse is a brick wall, signifying the barriers that you must overcome to attain enlightenment and experience true joy.

Card Meaning

The Sun represents success, achievement, and positivity. As an illuminator, it brings clarity and understanding to any challenges or obstacles you may encounter on your journey.

The Sun teaches you to celebrate your accomplishments and find joy in the simple pleasures of life. It reminds you to bask in the warmth of your achievements and to acknowledge your worth and contributions. Sometimes, the greatest warmth comes from within, through self-recognition and self-appreciation.

Affirmation

I am worthy of all the blessings that come my way.

Journal Prompts

★   Reflect on a time when you felt truly joyful and alive. What circumstances surrounded that experience? If you do not have any recent memories, how can you create more moments of joy in your life?

★ What are the areas of your life where you are experiencing success and abundance? Regardless of whether they are small or big wins, how can you express gratitude for these blessings?

★ Visualize yourself riding confidently into the future, guided by the light of the Sun. What dreams and aspirations do you wish to manifest? How can you align your actions with your vision to bring them into reality?

XX. Judgement

WAKE-UP CALL

Astrological Associations

Celestial Body
Pluto

Zodiac Sign
Scorpio

Keywords
Awakening, self-realization, accountability, redemption, karma, epiphany.

Understanding Judgement

Judgement depicts the Archangel Gabriel blowing a trumpet, representing a divine call to rise from the depths of the unconscious. The sound of the trumpet symbolizes an awakening, encouraging you to transcend your limitations and embrace a higher purpose. A man, woman, and child rise from their coffins, signifying the resurrection of the soul and the opportunity for spiritual renewal as you shed old beliefs, patterns, and attachments.

Card Meaning

Judgement represents a moment of awakening or self-realization. It symbolizes confronting past mistakes and taking accountability for your actions or decisions. It is that final "ah-ha!" moment as you near the completion of the Fool's Journey.

Judgement teaches you to forgive yourself and others, allowing your consciousness to expand and your spirit to evolve. With this higher understanding, you can embrace a fresh start.

Affirmation

I release my Judgement of myself and choose to forgive my past mistakes with compassion.

Journal Prompts

★   Think about a time of awakening or realization in your life. How did it impact your perception of yourself and the world around you?

★   Imagine it is time for you to face your judgement. What aspects of your life would you celebrate, and what aspects would you seek forgiveness or redemption for?

★   Look at the lessons you have learned from past mistakes. How
    did these experiences shape your character and contribute to
    your personal growth?

XXI. The World

I CAME, I SAW, I CONQUERED

Astrological Associations

Celestial Body
Saturn

Zodiac Signs
Taurus, Leo, Scorpio, Aquarius

Keywords
Completion, mastery, accomplishment, fulfillment.

Understanding the World

The World depicts a naked woman inside of a laurel wreath. She holds
two wands, reminiscent of the wand held by the Magician. The woman
is symbolic of the soul's journey. The laurel wreath represents ultimate
victory and achievement and looks like an ouroboros, symbolizing the
cyclical nature of life. She is surrounded by the four creatures from
the Wheel of Fortune representing the four fixed signs of the zodiac:
the lion (Leo), the bull (Taurus), the eagle (Scorpio), and the angel
(Aquarius). They are also the embodiment of the four suits of tarot:
Wands, Pentacles, Cups, and Swords.

Card Meaning

Congratulations! You have reached the end of your epic voyage
and have thus completed the Fool's Journey! The World represents
the culmination of a journey, symbolizing a sense of completion,
fulfillment, and integration. It signifies completing your goals
and aspirations.

The World teaches you to celebrate your achievements and embrace
your wholeness. It encourages you to reflect on the lessons you have
learned, the challenges you have overcome, and the growth you have
achieved. Remember to embrace closure and transition with openness
and acceptance, as every ending marks the beginning of a new chapter
in your story. Give yourself a well-deserved pat on the back and then
line back up at the starting line, as your upcoming new beginning is
bringing you back to the beginning of the tarot deck, the Fool.

Bang! goes the starting gun, and off you go, my dear Fool, on another
wild ride through the Fool's Journey. Let the adventure begin…again!

Affirmation

I am whole and complete.

Journal Prompts

★ Reflect on a significant life milestone that you have recently completed. How do you feel about reaching the end of this journey? What lessons have you learned along the way?

★ Consider the areas of your life where you feel a sense of fulfillment. What factors contribute to this feeling of wholeness? How can you nurture this feeling?

★ Explore any areas of your life where you still feel incomplete. What steps can you take to bring completion to these areas?

Part 3

The Fool's Guide to the Minor Arcana

CHAPTER 7

The Suit of Wands

"I want..."

Keywords

Passion, action, ambition, determination, power, adventure, confidence, spontaneity, travel.

Understanding the Suit of Wands

Welcome to the passionate realm of the Wands suit, where fiery passion, ambition, and enthusiasm set the stage for the next adventure on the Fool's Journey. The Wands are like magic wands, the kind you see in fairytales or movies with witches. Wands represent the passionate energy woven into our dreams and desires. By waving your wand in the air, you have a direct line to the cosmic energy, using it to weave your destiny and make things happen! Abracadabra!

The Wands are represented by the wand or staff, an ancient symbol of authority, power, and divine connection and is often carried by royalty. In tarot, wands have sprouting leaves, which symbolize the potential for new growth and manifesting desires. Because one wields a wand, they serve as a conduit for the dynamic energy of the universe and are used to bring things from thought to fruition.

In the realm of tarot, Wands represent the element of fire, which is symbolic of igniting a matchstick sparking ambition, motivation, and a sense of adventure from within. The wands burn bright and bring the intensity needed to accomplish your goals with gusto. This suit is dominated by the color red symbolizing power, passionate energy, courage, strength, and determination to pursue one's dreams.

As the Fool journeys through the Wands suit, they will encounter
a cast of characters that embody the essence of this vibrant energy
and situations that require them to pull from their inner power and
strength. From the fiery Ace of Wands to the triumphant King of
Wands, each card offers a unique perspective on the fiery aspects of
life, teaching you to embrace your passions and take bold action as you
step into your personal power.

Ace of Wands

LIGHT YOUR MATCH

Astrological Associations

Celestial Body
Mars

Zodiac Signs
Aries, Leo, Sagittarius

Keywords
Passion, inspiration, drive, action, energy, enthusiasm, spark.

Understanding the Ace of Wands

The Ace of Wands depicts a cloud with a hand reaching out offering you a wand with sprouting leaves. The hand is a representation of Spirit giving you an offering and bringing opportunity to embrace your unique talents and creative prowess. The budding wand represents the seed of inspiration and the spark that ignites passion, bursting into your reality with potential. It symbolizes new ideas and opportunities that need to be nurtured. The sprouting leaves symbolize the growth and expansion that the Fool can experience by acting on that spark and pursuing their passions. The leaves also form the Hebrew letter *Yod*, meaning "finger of God," symbolizing divine inspiration.

Card Meaning

The Ace of Wands represents a fresh start in pursuing your passions. It is the spark of inspiration and an opportunity to follow your inner fire and direct it toward achieving your aspirations.

The Ace of Wands invites you to seize the moment and channel your energy into pursuing your dreams. It symbolizes the beginning of a new project, or a surge of motivation, and the inner drive to manifest your desires into reality.

This Ace of Wands teaches you to trust your instincts, embrace your talents, and fearlessly begin a new, passionate journey. Allow yourself to see what is on the other side of your Fool's Journey.

Affirmation

I fearlessly pursue my passions.

Journal Prompts

★   What sparks your enthusiasm and sets your soul on fire?

★   What fears or doubts hold you back from pursuing your
    passions? How can you overcome them?

★   What steps can you take right now to manifest your passions
    into reality?

Two of Wands

EXPANDING YOUR WORLD

Astrological Associations

Celestial Body

Mars

Zodiac Sign

Aries

Keywords

Vision, choices, strategic planning, exploration.

Understanding the Two of Wands

The Two of Wands depicts a man holding a globe. The globe signifies an expanding perspective, vision, and the desire to explore uncharted territories or something new. The man carries the world in the palm of his hand while standing at the top of the castle he lives in. This is the Fool examining the life that he has achieved and the potential possibilities of pursuing a different path. He is contemplating his next move. The wand in his hand represents his power and the tools that he possesses to manifest his dreams if he chooses to wield his wand.

Card Meaning

The Two of Wands represents having to choose between different ideas or situations and embracing your ability to make important decisions.

While you waste time asking yourself, "Should I stay, or should I go?" opportunities may pass you by. Remember, my dear Fool, you hold the power (world) in your hands. Have the courage to travel outside your comfort zone and let the adventure unfold if you want to see the view from the other side.

Affirmation

I courageously leave my comfort zone to manifest my dreams.

Journal Prompts

★   What long-term goals or aspirations do you have?

★   What choices or decisions can you make to align with your long-term vision?

★   How can you overcome any fears or doubts that may be holding you back from taking the next step?

Three of Wands

SHIPS COMING IN

Astrological Associations

Celestial Body
Sun

Zodiac Sign
Aries

Keywords
Expansion, progress, foresight, ships coming in.

Understanding the Three of Wands

The Three of Wands depicts a man wearing a red robe, the color of passion and energy, standing on top of a cliff overlooking the sea. This is the man from the Two of Wands who has decided to come down from his castle, as he has made the choice to explore a new path. Ships sail in the sea, symbolizing that his world is expanding and his ships are coming in; however, there is no dock for him to moor his ships. He has just started manifesting his passions in the real world but has not yet ironed out the details. To help him complete his manifestation, he may need additional support represented by him leaning on the two wands behind him.

Card Meaning

The Three of Wands represents a period of expansion. It is the beginning of progress that occurs after establishing a strong foundation.

The Three of Wands is a reminder to embrace the excitement of new possibilities and to take calculated risks to reach your goals. It is important to trust your instincts, expand on your past successes, and have confidence in your ability to navigate uncharted territory.

Affirmation

I venture into the unknown to expand my horizons and create future possibilities.

Journal Prompts

★ What new opportunities are on the horizon that you are excited for?

★ How can you continue building on your past achievements to move yourself forward?

★ How can you collaborate or partner with someone to support your growth?

Four of Wands

REACHING A MILESTONE

Astrological Associations

Celestial Body
Venus

Zodiac Sign
Aries

Keywords
Celebrating milestones, fruition, stable foundation, homecoming.

Understanding the Four of Wands

The Four of Wands depicts a celebratory scene with two individuals holding a bouquet of flowers, while standing under an archway. The two individuals symbolize a union, partnership, or the sharing of an accomplishment. There is a crowd of people who have gathered behind them to celebrate and cheer them on.

Card Meaning

The Four of Wands represents celebrating a milestone or a minor success. It is a small victory and symbolizes a sense of accomplishment.

The Four of Wands encourages you to recognize your efforts and teaches the importance of acknowledging your small victories and enjoying the fruits of your labor with the loved ones around you.

Affirmation

I celebrate my milestones with joy and gratitude.

Journal Prompts

★   What is the most recent life milestone you have completed?

★   What foundation did you create to help you achieve this milestone?

★   How would you improve this foundation to better equip you to reach your next milestone?

Five of Wands

CLASH OF EGOS

Astrological Associations

Celestial Body
Saturn

Zodiac Sign
Leo

Keywords
Competition, rivalry, adversity, tension, clash of egos.

Understanding the Five of Wands

The Five of Wands depicts five young boys engaged in conflict and using their wands to fight. Their youth suggests that they are sparring instead of fighting. As wands represent passion, this conflict symbolizes a clash in passionate energies and egos. The wielding wands represent assertiveness and the desire to be seen and heard.

> **Study Tip:** Notice that the boys are fighting with wands, not swords. Everyone is getting banged up a little, but no one is being cut. It is a conflict, but not a war.

Card Meaning

Drama, drama, drama! The Five of Wands represents a difference in opinions and the need to be assertive. It is the battle of wills and egos clashing.

The Five of Wands teaches you to navigate conflict and encourages you to assert yourself while standing up for your beliefs. Through this practice, you continue to evolve as you must expand your perspective to understand another's view.

Affirmation

I advocate for myself during times when I am challenged.

Journal Prompts

★   Reflect on a recent time when someone challenged your opinion. What did you learn from that experience?

★   How do you typically respond when people disagree with you? How can you advocate for yourself better during moments of debate?

★ Are there any recurring patterns in how you respond to a disagreement? Do you agree with the new argument, defend your argument, or withdraw your argument? Is there growth to be had in this area? If so, how?

Six of Wands

BASK IN THE GLORY

Astrological Associations

Celestial Body
Jupiter

Zodiac Sign
Leo

Keywords
Victory, recognition, achievement, public acclaim.

Understanding the Six of Wands

The Six of Wands depicts a man riding triumphantly on a white horse. He carries a wand in his hand with a laurel wreath attached. A crowd of cheering people gather in support to welcome him, and each supporter carries their own wand. The white horse symbolizes purity, strength, and nobility and the laurel wreath symbolizes victory and success. The cheering crowd symbolizes public recognition of his achievements.

Card Meaning

It is time to strike a pose and take a victory lap because the Six of Wands represents a well-deserved victory and the recognition that comes with it. It is your red-carpet moment, so bask in the glory and let the world applaud your greatness.

The Six of Wands teaches you the importance of not only celebrating but also acknowledging your successes. It is time to recognize the hard work and dedication that got you to your present moment.

This is an opportunity to embrace your confidence and take pride in yourself, as your success may inspire others.

Affirmation

I confidently embrace recognition and use my success to motivate and inspire others.

Journal Prompts

★   What strengths and qualities contributed to your success? How can you further nurture and develop these qualities?

★   How can you use your achievements as a source of inspiration and motivation for others?

★   Are there any challenges or obstacles you overcame on your
    path to success? How did they shape you?

Seven of Wands

STAND YOUR GROUND

Astrological Associations

Celestial Body
Mars

Zodiac Sign
Leo

Keywords
Standing your ground, perseverance, resilience, defiance.

Understanding the Seven of Wands

The Seven of Wands depicts a man standing on a hill. He is wielding his wand while looking down at six people with opposing wands. The wands the opposing people hold symbolize challenges, obstacles, and opposing viewpoints. The man's elevated position on the hill symbolizes a sense of self-assuredness and strength. His firm stance and raised wand symbolize his defiance and determination. This is the Fool engaged in a moment of conflict requiring him to stand his ground and stand up for his beliefs.

The Fool has lost a piece of his shoe (see the Fool) while holding firm to his convictions, suggesting the struggle has been difficult. Still, he continues to stand tall and assert his boundaries in the face of adversity while completing the Fool's Journey.

Card Meaning

The Seven of Wands represents the need to rise above challenges and assert your position. It is a time of challenges and competition, during which you must defend your position or beliefs.

The Seven of Wands teaches you to stand your ground and defend your turf. It is like being surrounded by a pack of hungry wolves but choosing not to back down. It reminds you to trust in your strength by standing up for what you believe in and fighting for what is yours. So, wield your wand confidently and show 'em who is boss!

Affirmation

I stand tall and strong, defending my beliefs and boundaries with unwavering determination.

Journal Prompts

★ Reflect on a recent situation where you had to defend your beliefs or stand up for yourself. How did it make you feel?

★   What values or principles are worth defending in your life?
     How can you strengthen your commitment to them?

★   Are there any fears or doubts that hold you back from asserting
     yourself? How can you overcome them?

Eight of Wands

THE NEED FOR SPEED

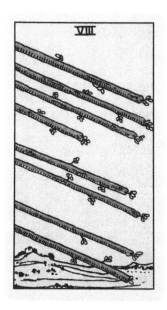

Astrological Associations

Celestial Body
Mercury

Zodiac Sign
Sagittarius

Keywords
Action, fast movement, opportunities, travel.

Understanding the Eight of Wands

The Eight of Wands depicts eight wands soaring through the sky, symbolizing fast movement and progress. As wands symbolize fire, passion, and action, the flying wands represent the energy of advancement and a multitude of opportunities coming toward the Fool. Their rapid movement symbolizes the need to act swiftly and seize the moment. The clear sky and absence of obstacles indicate smooth and unhindered progression.

Card Meaning

Zoom, zoom, zoom! The Eight of Wands is a cosmic rollercoaster ride, with wands flying at lightning speed, and it represents a surge of forward movement and the rapid manifestation of your desires. It symbolizes that things are moving quickly in your favor, bringing about new opportunities and exciting developments. The fast movement of the wands also signifies travel.

The Eight of Wands teaches you about swift action and making quick decisions. Be open to new opportunities that come and be proactive about pursuing your goals. Just remember to hold onto your hat during the process!

Affirmation

I embrace the opportunities that come my way and take decisive action to manifest my desires.

Journal Prompts

★   What areas of your life are currently in a state of acceleration and progress? How can you further capitalize on these opportunities?

★   Are there any projects or goals that require your immediate
    attention? How can you take swift action to move
    them forward?

★   How can you maintain balance and focus amidst the fast-paced
    nature of your life? Are there any areas where you need to slow
    down or prioritize?

Nine of Wands

A WARRIOR SPIRIT

Astrological Associations

Celestial Body
Moon

Zodiac Sign
Sagittarius

Keywords
The final push, inner strength, stamina, determination, defensiveness.

Understanding the Nine of Wands

The Nine of Wands depicts a determined man standing tall with a bandaged head. He is holding a wand in a defensive stance. Although wounded, he now has a full pair of shoes again (see the Seven of Wands). This symbolizes the culmination of a challenging journey full of obstacles and setbacks. The bandages cover battle scars the Fool received during lessons learned from past experiences. He is ready to face future challenges to protect his achievements.

Card Meaning

The Nine of Wands represents determination while facing obstacles. It symbolizes that this is a time when you need to have the inner strength required to persevere.

You have been through the wringer, but you are still standing tall. The Nine of Wands is like climbing a mountain, only to find another one waiting for you. Do not stop now as the number nine is near the number ten, which represents the completion of a journey. You are nearly there, so take a deep breath, gather your strength, and give one final push forward. You are almost done!

Affirmation

I embrace the challenges that come my way, knowing they make me stronger.

Journal Prompts

★ Identify the boundaries you need to set in your life to protect your well-being and goals. How can you communicate and reinforce those boundaries?

★ Are there any limiting beliefs or self-doubt that you need to overcome? How can you build your confidence and reinforce your inner strength?

★   How can you support others in their journey to become more
     resilient? How can you share your experiences and lessons to
     inspire and encourage others?

Ten of Wands

RELEASING YOUR BURDENS

Astrological Associations

Celestial Body
Saturn

Zodiac Sign
Sagittarius

Keywords
Burden, overwhelm, struggle, release.

Understanding the Ten of Wands

The Ten of Wands depicts a man unsuccessfully carrying a heavy load of ten wands. The man's strained posture represents the weight and struggle that comes from carrying too much. The ten wands symbolize each of the responsibilities, commitments, and burdens that have accumulated over time. He is exhausted and is struggling to move forward. The distant village represents the destination or the desired outcome after releasing the burdens.

Card Meaning

The Ten of Wands represents feeling burdened and overwhelmed by the weight of responsibilities due to biting off more than you can chew. It is like carrying a heavy load on your back, causing you to feel the weight of the world.

The Ten of Wands teaches you the importance of releasing responsibilities that no longer serve you or align with your goals or well-being. Invite in liberation by remembering that it is okay to ask for help. You do not need to be a wand-hoarding hero.

Affirmation

I release the burdens that weigh me down and embrace my liberation.

Journal Prompts

★ Identify the specific responsibilities or commitments that feel burdensome in your life. How are they impacting your well-being and overall sense of freedom?

★ Reflect on the reasons why you took on these burdens. Are they still relevant and aligned with your current goals and values?

★ Imagine a life free from overwhelming burdens. What would it look like? What steps can you take to move closer to that vision?

The Royal Family: Wands Court Cards

Wands Court Family Emblem

Salamander
In the tarot, the salamander is associated with the element of fire and represents resilience and adaptability. A salamander can regenerate its limbs, which symbolizes its ability to overcome adversity.

The family emblem can be seen on the clothes and thrones of the Wands Court.

Astrological Associations
The Wands Court embodies all fire signs—Aries, Leo, and Sagittarius.

Understanding the Wands Court
Welcome to the blazing Court of Wands—the Avengers of the tarot world! The Royal Family of Wands rules over the realm of passionate energy, inspiration, and action. Each member of the royal family in the Wands Court carries the spirit of ambition and adventure and symbolizes different aspects of fiery energy. They are the explorers, the

go-getters, the risk-takers, the visionaries, the charismatic leaders, and the flame-keepers who know how to stoke their inner fire.

Picture this: the Wands suit is the raging bonfire at a party, and the Wands Court are the guests who RSVPed with a "Hell yeah!" These firecrackers take pride in reigning over action and passion with enthusiasm and light up your life with their sizzling presence when they make an appearance in your reading. They have that magnetic charm that draws people in like moths to a flame and are the life of the party and the heart of the action. But most importantly, they know how to get things done. The Wands Court are feisty, fierce, and not afraid to get their hands dirty. Their role is to inspire you, to push you beyond your limits, and to ignite that drive within you. They teach you to embrace your authenticity to make a significant impact in your life and the world around you.

The Wands Court can represent actual people, such as family members, friends, or other people encountered in daily interactions. The cards can also represent people in certain professions that require trailblazers, such as entrepreneurs, innovators, entertainers, business consultants, managers, and CEOs who know how to motivate and inspire teams. It is your wheelers and dealers or people slinging contracts and bulldozing through negotiations. The Wands Court also embodies the spirit of adventure and exploration and involves professions that include travel.

As we delve into the realm of the Wands Court, we are reminded that we have the power to manifest our desires and these powerful archetypes guide the Fool on a transformative journey of self-realization and empowerment.

Page of Wands

STOKE YOUR INNER FIRE

Keywords

Curiosity, inspiration, enthusiasm, exploration, spontaneity.

Understanding the Page of Wands

The Page of Wands is a pre-adolescent member of the Wands Royal Family and is depicted as a young, energetic girl who is just beginning to explore and discover her territory. She holds a wand, which symbolizes the awakening of her passions and her readiness to embark on new adventures.

Card Meaning

The Page of Wands represents an influx of energy and symbolizes exploring new passions. It is a burst of inspiration that can lead to an exciting opportunity that sparks your curiosity.

The Page of Wands teaches you to embrace your childlike curiosity and spontaneity and allow it to guide you. It encourages you to tap into your creative potential while you explore new interests and fearlessly pursue your passions.

Affirmation

I fearlessly embark on exciting adventures and let my creativity flow freely.

Journal Prompts

★   Reflect on a recent moment of inspiration or a new idea that sparked your curiosity. How did it make you feel, and what steps can you take to explore it further?

★   Consider a situation where spontaneity led to a positive outcome or a memorable experience. How can you incorporate more spontaneity into your life?

★   Imagine yourself as the Page of Wands, ready to embark on a new adventure. What qualities do you embody, and what exciting opportunities lie ahead?

Knight of Wands

UNLEASH YOUR ADVENTUROUS SPIRIT

Keywords

Action, adventure, ambition, impulsiveness.

Understanding the Knight of Wands

The Knight of Wands is an adolescent member of the Wands Royal Family and is depicted as a mounted knight charging ahead with a wand. The galloping horse represents drive, ambition, and fearlessly moving forward. The wand the knight holds symbolizes the energy driving his passions. The salamander on his clothing represents transformation and adaptability as he navigates new challenges.

Card Meaning

The Knight of Wands represents taking risks, pursuing your passions, and following your heart's desires. It is the bold and charismatic daredevil, ready to charge into the unknown.

The Knight of Wands teaches you the importance of fearlessly exploring new territories while tapping into the things that drive you. It encourages you to be bold, trust your abilities to overcome obstacles, step out of your comfort zone, and embody the courage needed to manifest your desires.

Affirmation

I am the embodiment of limitless potential.

Journal Prompts

★ What dreams and desires ignite a fire within you? How can you take action toward manifesting them?

★ Consider the challenges or obstacles that have been holding you back from pursuing your passions. How can you overcome them and move forward with courage and determination?

★ Identify one area of your life where you have been playing it safe or holding back. How can you inject more passion, adventure, and excitement into that area?

Queen of Wands

REIGN WITH CONFIDENCE

Keywords

Confidence, determination, magnetism, independence.

Understanding the Queen of Wands

The Queen of Wands depicts a woman of authority sitting on a throne.
She embodies fierce confidence and rules with power and grace.
She reigns with her wand of power and passion, giving her a strong
presence that commands attention and inspires onlookers. The black
cat at her feet symbolizes intuition, mysticism, and the hidden depths
of her personality. She is a natural-born leader, unafraid to express her
creativity and pursue her passions.

Card Meaning

The Queen of Wands represents the epitome of passion, charisma, and magnetic charm. She symbolizes confidence and the ability to inspire others with her vision.

The Queen of Wands teaches you the importance of harnessing your own power, embracing your authenticity, and leading with authority. She encourages you to honor your passions by expressing your unique talents and unapologetically shining your light.

Affirmation

I inspire others by confidently expressing my unique gifts to the world.

Journal Prompts

★ Reflect on moments when you have felt most confident and powerful in your life. What qualities did you embody during those times, and how can you bring more of that energy into your present life?

★ Consider the passions and talents that make you truly unique. How can you express them more fully and confidently in your personal and professional life?

★ Imagine yourself as the Queen of Wands, leading with charisma and inspiring those around you. How would you use your power to make a positive impact in your community or sphere of influence?

King of Wands

SET THE WORLD ABLAZE

Keywords

Leadership, charisma, vision, action.

Understanding the King of Wands

The King of Wands depicts a man sitting on a throne. His throne
symbolizes authority and leadership. The wand he holds represents
his power and the salamander on his robe and throne symbolizes his
transformation and ability to overcome the challenges needed to reach
his goals. Looking similar to the man in the Two of Wands, he is the
Fool who now overlooks the new world he has created for himself after
taking the initial risk. He is no longer the Two of Wands; he is now the
King of Wands.

Card Meaning

The King of Wands represents the ultimate visionary leader. He is the CEO of the Wand Court. This card symbolizes taking bold action, embracing your unique vision, and inspiring others to follow your lead.

The King of Wands encourages you to own your power and step into your role as a visionary leader.

Affirmation

I harness my creative fire to make a positive impact in the world.

Journal Prompts

★ Reflect on any doubts or insecurities that may be holding you back from fully embracing your leadership potential. How can you overcome those barriers and step into your role as a confident and visionary leader?

★ Reflect on moments when you have felt most confident and powerful in a leadership role. What qualities did you embody during those times, and how can you channel those qualities into your present life?

★ Identify one area of your life where you would like to make a significant impact. What steps can you take to assert your authority, inspire others, and create positive change in that area?

CHAPTER 8

The Suit of Cups

"I feel..."

Keywords

Emotions, heartstrings, relationships, romance, imagination, dreams, creativity.

Understanding the Suit of Cups

Welcome to the enchanting world of the Cups suit, where emotions, intuition, and the depths of the soul flow like a river…or rather a broken dam. It is like getting caught in a hurricane of fuzzy feelings, love (sometimes unrequited), joy and sadness, and a whole lot of drama. The suit of cups represents the progression of the emotional journey while highlighting the highest of highs and gutter lows of the heart space. Cups symbolize the overall emotional experience in a situation by revealing your deepest feelings and desires associated with love, relationships, and overall fulfillment. Cups can also reveal the inevitable emotional blockage, emotional immaturity, and the areas in life where you may be emotionally unmanaged.

The Cups are represented by the chalice or cup, a sacred vessel that holds the magical elixir of emotions and spiritual insight. Cups usually overflow with water, which symbolizes the abundance of love, compassion, and intuition available to you.

In the realm of tarot, this suit represents the element of water, symbolic of the ebb and flow of emotions. It invites you to dive into the waters of your feelings and explore the depths of your subconscious. The colors blue and turquoise of the suit represent the peace and serenity cups can offer when you are in a state of emotional balance and symbolize the harmony that comes with healing.

When traveling through the Cups suit, you can find solace in the tides of life and bask in the profound beauty of the thing that makes us all humans—emotions. Let the journey of the heart begin!

Ace of Cups

OPEN YOUR HEART

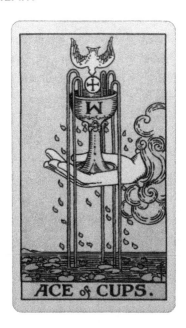

Astrological Associations

Celestial Body
Moon

Zodiac Signs
Cancer, Scorpio, Pisces

Keywords
A new emotional beginning, love, intuition.

Understanding the Ace of Cups

The Ace of Cups depicts a cloud with a hand reaching out offering you a cup that is full of water. This is an opportunity to work toward emotional fulfillment. The hand is a representation of Spirit giving you an offering, which brings an opportunity of love (familial, platonic, and romantic), the chance to activate your heart center, and the ability to enhance your imagination. On top of the card is a dove, a symbol of the Holy Spirit and the divine, dropping an offering into the cup that is presented to you. The water droplets form the shape of the Hebrew letter *Yod*, meaning the "finger of God," symbolizing that this is divine love.

Card Meaning

The Ace of Cups represents new emotional beginnings. It symbolizes a new chapter in your life that is full of the potential for love, happiness, and emotional fulfillment.

The Ace of Cups teaches you to open your heart to possibility. The universe is trying to give you the opportunity of emotional expansion, but this requires you to be ready to receive.

Affirmation

I open my heart to love and allow it to flow abundantly in my life.

Journal Prompts

★ What is the definition of emotional fulfillment for you?

★ How can you become more receptive to love and compassion?

★ What fresh emotional starts are you encountering in your life?

Two of Cups

THE EXCHANGE OF OFFERS

Astrological Associations

Celestial Body
Venus

Zodiac Sign
Cancer

Keywords
Partnership, contracts, union, communication.

Understanding the Two of Cups

The Two of Cups depicts two people holding cups, participating in an exchange by offering their cups to one another. This exchange has an emotional significance that tugs on the heart center and symbolizes the beginning of a relationship or partnership. There is a caduceus (the thing that looks like a medical sign), the symbol of the Greek god Hermes, considered a messenger of the gods, and a lion attached to mercurial wings, which represents the communication needed to form fruitful partnerships.

Card Meaning

The Two of Cups represents mutual love, a union, and a connection that brings balance and harmony. It may also represent a negotiation or a contract exchange as there are two people offering their cup, while also assessing the other person's cup to see what is in it.

The Two of Cups teaches you about the importance of connection. Opportunities are often presented by other people. This encourages you to put yourself out there to make yourself available for these opportunities.

Affirmation

I am open to deep connections and soulful partnerships.

Journal Prompts

★   Think about a relationship in your life that has been meaningful. What have you learned from it?

★   How can you maintain a balance in showing and receiving love in your relationships?

★   What does it mean to you to have a harmonious and collaborative partnership?

Three of Cups

A JOYOUS CELEBRATION

Astrological Associations

Celestial Body
Mercury

Zodiac Sign
Cancer

Keywords
Celebration, friendship, joy, community.

Understanding the Three of Cups

The Three of Cups depicts three women dancing, sharing a drink, and clinking their cups. The bottom of the card depicts a lot of fruit or an abundant harvest. The fruit symbolizes that they have reaped what they have sown. The women are celebrating that there is fruit in their labor and are sharing a drink because there is enough to go around!

Card Meaning

When the Three of Cups shows up, it is time to party! The Three of Cups represents celebration, joy, friendships, and overall good vibes. It symbolizes a time of happiness and socializing with loved ones. This card may also represent events or large gatherings, such as a birthday party or anniversary celebration.

The Three of Cups teaches you it is okay to live a little and celebrate your accomplishments along the way. You do not have to wait for a culmination of achievements to give yourself a pat on the back.

Affirmation

I celebrate the joy of friendship and cherish the bonds I share with others.

Journal Prompts

★   Describe a joyful and celebratory moment in your life. How did it make you feel?

★   How can you cultivate a sense of friendship and camaraderie in your social circles?

★   What role does community play in supporting your emotional well-being?

Four of Cups

TAKING THINGS FOR GRANTED

Astrological Associations

Celestial Body
Moon

Zodiac Sign
Cancer

Keywords
Apathy, taking things for granted, contemplation, missed opportunities.

Understanding the Four of Cups

The Four of Cups depicts a man sitting beneath a tree assessing his cup. He pouts while folding his arms across his chest representing that he is not happy with the cups that are currently in his possession. Once again, a hand is reaching out from a cloud with an offering of another cup; however, the man is too consumed with his current situation to notice the blessing that the Spirit is trying to give him. This man is apathetic toward his current circumstances and is experiencing dissatisfaction. He has three full cups but cannot see the gifts presented to him in his life.

Card Meaning

The Four of Cups represents contemplation, which is usually apathetic in nature. It is like a teenager rolling their eyes at life. That all-too-familiar feeling of "meh." It is the Fool, missing an opportunity floating by because he is too busy pouting to notice.

The Four of Cups teaches you to take some time to reflect on your emotions and what is truly important in life. Is there another way to view your current circumstances? Are you taking things for granted?

Affirmation

I choose to see the blessings that surround me and appreciate what I have.

Journal Prompts

★ Explore a time when you felt emotionally stagnant or dissatisfied. What lessons did you learn from that experience?

★ How can you cultivate gratitude and appreciation for the blessings in your life?

★ What opportunities for emotional growth are you overlooking?

Five of Cups

GRIEVING A LOSS

Astrological Associations

Celestial Body
Mars

Zodiac Sign
Scorpio

Keywords
Disappointment, sadness, regret, grief, loss.

Understanding the Five of Cups

The Five of Cups depicts a man mourning over his three cups that have spilled. He is sad and looks at his spilled cups with disappointment and grief. He has faced the loss of his cups or the loss of something or someone that was near and dear to him. With his back turned against the remaining two cups, he has also lost sight of what remains. Unlike the Four of Cups, where the man takes his cups for granted, in the Five of Cups, the man cannot see his cups due to heavy disappointment or sadness. The Five of Cups acknowledges that you may be hurting emotionally, which is represented by the river flowing, but that all is not lost. The Fool's Journey is not complete as there is more waiting for him in the city behind him. He needs to cross that bridge to make it to the other side.

Card Meaning

The Five of Cups represents disappointment and loss and suggests that you may be experiencing emotional pain and sadness. But chin up, buttercup! Look around, and you might spot those two remaining cups waiting behind you. What was that saying about not crying over spilled milk?

The Five of Cups teaches you to keep pushing forward. It is okay to feel disappointed as life is a series of ups and downs. Just make sure you get back up.

Affirmation

I focus on the positive aspects of my life and find strength in moments of adversity.

Journal Prompts

★   Reflect on a significant loss or disappointment in your life. How did it shape you?

★   How can you find healing and forgiveness in the face of
    emotional pain?

★   What practices or resources can support you in navigating
    through grief and loss?

Six of Cups

REMEMBERING THE PAST

Astrological Associations

Celestial Body
Sun

Zodiac Sign
Scorpio

Keywords
Nostalgia, memories, innocence.

Understanding the Six of Cups

The Six of Cups depicts two children playing in a garden full of
flowers. The children offer a cup full of flowers to each other,
representing generosity demonstrated through the act of giving and
receiving. The cup symbolizes embracing your inner child while
finding joy in the little things. The Six of Cups is the next step of the
Fool's Journey, as it is common to reflect on pleasing memories after
suffering a loss in the Five of Cups.

Card Meaning

The Six of Cups represents nostalgia and memories and suggests
you are feeling sentimental or thinking of the past. It can symbolize
reconnecting with family or old friends, revisiting past interests
or hobbies that brought joy and fulfillment, or rekindling a
romantic relationship.

The Six of Cups teaches you to stop and smell the roses and to
remember the sweeter times in life. Embrace the inner child that used
to play in the dirt and allow them to come out to play periodically. Life
does not always have to be so serious.

Affirmation

*I embrace the innocence and wonder of my inner child, allowing it
to guide me.*

Journal Prompts

★   Recall a nostalgic memory from your childhood. How does it
     influence your present emotions?

★   How can you foster a sense of innocence and playfulness in
     your daily life?

★   What patterns from the past might be impacting your
     current relationships?

Seven of Cups

CHOICES

Astrological Associations

Celestial Body
Venus

Zodiac Sign
Scorpio

Keywords
Choices, decision-making, opportunity, illusions, daydreaming, emotional confusion.

Understanding the Seven of Cups

The Seven of Cups depicts seven cups, each filled with a different object: a man, a ghost, a snake, a castle, jewels, a laurel wreath, and a dragon. The shadowy figure is the Fool assessing what is being offered in each cup and deciding which one to pick. This imagery represents being faced with a choice between different options and that each option is equally enticing but may not necessarily be what it seems. Whereas the Ace of Cups offers one cup extending from a cloud, the Seven of Cups offers multiple cups, which symbolize opportunities and manifestations. The Fool must be careful not to fall victim to possible illusions in front of him, as not all cups offer good things.

Card Meaning

The Seven of Cups represents choices and possibilities. But beware, as it also symbolizes your daydreams and illusions that are created using the power of your imagination.

The Seven of Cups teaches you to keep your feet on the ground and choose your dreams wisely. That unicorn ranch might not be as practical as it sounds. In the words of my late, great mother, "All that glitters ain't gold."

Affirmation

I clarify my desires and focus on what truly matters.

Journal Prompts

★ Take some time to delve into your dreams, desires, and fantasies. What emotions do they stir up within you?

★ How can you differentiate between what is real and what is not when it comes to your emotional experiences?

★ What actions can you take to bring your heartfelt wishes and aspirations to life?

Eight of Cups

MOVING ON

Astrological Associations

Celestial Body
Saturn

Zodiac Sign
Pisces

Keywords
Moving on, breaking up, emotional detachment, soul-searching.

Understanding the Eight of Cups

The Eight of Cups depicts a man walking away from eight cups in the middle of the night. Each cup is upright, and nothing has spilled, representing that he once found emotional fulfillment and satisfaction with these cups but has realized that they no longer serve him. The sun is not out to illuminate his path, so he does not know what lies ahead; however, he knows with his heart that he must go anyway. Instead, he will use the moon's glow to find his way. His hike up the mountain symbolizes that even though the decision is difficult, it is necessary for his emotional fulfillment.

Card Meaning

Ah, the breakup card! A poor sight to see if you are asking about the person you just met on Tinder. So, you hope this relationship can go the distance? Not if this card shows up! The Eight of Cups represents moving on and letting go. It suggests you need to leave behind something or *someone* no longer serving you.

The Eight of Cups teaches you to walk away from emotional baggage and seek a fresh start. It takes courage to leave behind things that you used to love, but you must understand more cups are waiting for you.

Affirmation

I bravely let go of what no longer serves me.

Journal Prompts

★ Reflect on a time when you walked away from a situation or a relationship for your emotional well-being. What lessons did you learn from that experience?

★ How can you honor your inner truth and prioritize your emotional needs?

★   What current emotions or attachments do you need to release
     to find greater fulfillment?

Nine of Cups

A WISH GRANTED

Astrological Associations

Celestial Body
Jupiter

Zodiac Sign
Pisces

Keywords
Wish granted, fulfillment, contentment.

Understanding the Nine of Cups

The Nine of Cups depicts a plump and happy man who has eaten and is satisfied. He sits proudly and is surrounded by his cups, which he displays like trophies. All nine cups sit full and upright. He is content and emotionally fulfilled.

Card Meaning

The Nine of Cups represents that your wishes are being granted. It is often referred to as the "wish card" and symbolizes emotional fulfillment and contentment.

The Nine of Cups teaches you how to embrace the pleasures of life and surround yourself with your heart's desires. It is difficult to experience abundance if you do not allow yourself to enjoy what you already have.

Affirmation

I deserve happiness and allow myself to experience deep satisfaction.

Journal Prompts

★   Identify three things that bring you pure joy and satisfaction. How often do you prioritize them in your life? Explore ways to incorporate more of these elements into your daily routine.

★   Consider the relationships in your life. Are there any connections that bring you genuine happiness and fulfillment? If so, how can you nurture and deepen those bonds? If not, how can you cultivate healthier relationships?

★   Reflect on a recent accomplishment or milestone. What steps did you take to achieve this, and how can you build upon this success in other areas of your life?

Ten of Cups

BLESSINGS AND HARMONY

Astrological Associations

Celestial Body
Mars

Zodiac Sign
Pisces

Keywords
Bliss, happy family life, harmony.

Understanding the Ten of Cups

The Ten of Cups depicts a loving family gathered under a rainbow of cups, which represents the culmination and completion of an emotional journey. The children playing in the garden of the Six of Cups appear in this card, symbolizing the need to reflect on the past and honor the journey required to reach this stage.

Card Meaning

The Ten of Cups represents emotional abundance, joy, and happiness in relationships. It symbolizes the achievement of hopes and dreams and is a reminder that abundance is a birthright.

The Ten of Cups teaches you to prioritize your emotional well-being, find happiness and fulfillment in your relationships, and remember that true wealth lies in the quality of your connections with others.

Affirmation

I am grateful for the abundance of love and joy in my life, and I attract more of it every day.

Journal Prompts

★ Describe your vision of emotional fulfillment and happiness. How can you align your life with that vision?

★ How can you nurture and create a loving and harmonious home environment?

★ What actions can you take to strengthen the emotional bonds within your family or chosen community?

The Royal Family: Cups Court Cards

Cups Court Family Emblem

Fish

In the tarot, a fish is associated with the element of water and represents your emotions, intuition, and subconscious. Fish invite you to look inward and explore what you are feeling.

The family emblem can be seen on the clothes and thrones of the Cups Court.

Astrological Associations

The Cups Court embodies all water signs—Cancer, Scorpio, and Pisces.

Understanding the Cups Court

Welcome to the enchanting realm of the Cups Court, where emotions flow like a river and matters of the heart take center stage. From the youthful and spirited to the wise and regal, these court cards offer us a glimpse into the intricate tapestry of human emotions and relationships.

In the Cups Court resides what I call the Royal Family of Cups, who rule over emotions and the element of water. Within this courtly family are characters who represent the essence of love, compassion, imagination, and creativity. They are powerful archetypes, guiding the Fool through the ever-changing tides of emotions and relationships. The wisdom and insights of the cards encourage the Fool to delve into their emotional depths, fostering a deeper understanding of self and their connections with others.

The Cups Court can represent actual people, such as family members, friends, or other people encountered in daily interactions. The cards can also represent people in certain professions, such as mental health professionals, social workers, artists, musicians, spiritual healers, psychics, astrologers, or other similar roles.

Page of Cups

CREATIVE BEGINNINGS

Keywords

Emotional immaturity, a message related to emotions, intuition, creativity, artistic expression.

Understanding the Page of Cups

The Page of Cups is the pre-adolescent member of the Cups Royal Family, bringing an aspect of emotional immaturity to a situation. This card depicts a young girl holding a cup or chalice, dressed in colorful clothing, standing in front of a large body of water. The body of water has high waves representing emotions that have not yet been mastered. The Page of Cups has just begun learning to manage and understand her emotions. The fish symbolizes fertility or the birth of something new in the realm of emotions. She admires the fish as she recognizes the feelings it provokes.

Card Meaning

The Page of Cups can indicate a message related to emotions, signify a new emotional beginning, or represent a sensitive or creative person. It symbolizes embracing a childlike sense of wonder and curiosity.

The Page of Cups teaches you to embrace emotional exploration and creativity, encouraging you to approach life with openness and curiosity. Be receptive to new experiences and express your emotions authentically, even if they may seem unfamiliar or overwhelming at times.

Affirmation

I express my emotions freely and authentically.

Journal Prompts

★   Which creative endeavors bring you joy and inspiration?

★   What subconscious messages or signs are you currently receiving?

★   How can you take care of your sensitivity and emotional well-being?

Knight of Cups

KNIGHT IN SHINING ARMOR

Keywords

Emotional pursuit, dreamy idealism, romance, charm, chivalry.

Understanding the Knight of Cups

The Knight of Cups is an adolescent member of the royal family and is depicted as a young man on a white horse, holding the cup of emotions and feelings in his hand. The white horse is not in a gallop, but instead a slow walk to prevent him from spilling his emotions in the cup. It is a measured and mature approach for preserving emotions after learning from being the previously emotionally vulnerable Page of Cups.

Card Meaning

The Knight of Cups is the hopeless romantic of the tarot. They ride in on their majestic steed, daydreaming about love and serenading their crushes with poetic verses. It represents a romantic, chivalrous, and idealistic person who has learned to identify their emotions but still has not mastered them. It also symbolizes chasing after your heart's desires.

The Knight of Cups teaches you to balance your emotions and actions. How many times have you gotten yourself into a pickle due to an emotional outburst?

Affirmation

I follow my heart's calling and pursue my dreams with passion and courage.

Journal Prompts

★ Reflect on a time when you followed your heart's desires without hesitation. How did it make you feel? What did you learn from that experience?

★ Explore your relationship with vulnerability. What does it mean to you, and how comfortable are you with expressing your emotions openly?

★ Think about a person who embodies the qualities of the Knight of Cups. What specific traits do you admire in them, and how can you incorporate those traits into your life?

Queen of Cups

INTUITIVE WISDOM

Keywords

Emotional maturity, intuition, compassion, empathy.

Understanding the Queen of Cups

The Queen of Cups is depicted as a regal and serene woman, holding the ultimate chalice of emotions, symbolizing her connection to her feelings, intuition, and subconscious mind. Unlike the Page of Cups, who had high waves in the body of water behind her, the Queen of Cups' water is calm, representing emotional maturity. The cliffs represent the challenging nature of her emotional journey; however, she has reached the top.

Card Meaning

This card represents emotional maturity and compassion. It also symbolizes the need to understand and empathize with others without judgement or criticism.

The Queen of Cups teaches you to confront obstacles with courage and perseverance, knowing that you have the emotional resources to overcome adversity and emerge stronger.

Affirmation

I am in touch with my emotions and allow my intuition to guide me in making wise decisions.

Journal Prompts

★ Reflect on a time when you fully embraced your nurturing and compassionate nature. How did it impact your relationships and the people around you?

★ Explore your intuition and psychic abilities. How do you recognize and trust your intuitive guidance? Are there any instances where your intuition has guided you in making important decisions?

★ Reflect on a time when you experienced emotional resilience and overcame a challenging situation. What strengths and coping mechanisms did you rely on, and how did they contribute to your growth?

King of Cups

EMOTIONAL MASTERY

Keywords
Emotional stability, leadership, wisdom, diplomatic.

Understanding the King of Cups
The King of Cups is depicted as a mature man sitting on a throne floating in the middle of the sea. His waters are choppy, representing the trials and tribulations that have occurred over the course of his life. He demonstrates that he has mastered his emotions by sitting on top of the water. He grips his cup tightly as he works to prevent his emotions from spilling, symbolizing emotional stability. A ship sails behind him, signifying his ability to maintain control over his emotions despite

inner turmoil. He is the master of his ship and leads and guides his kingdom despite his emotional state.

Card Meaning

This card represents emotional wisdom, maturity, and emotional stability. It symbolizes being in control of your emotions and not being easily influenced by external factors.

The King of Cups teaches you to trust your instincts instead of listening to others to make decisions that are right for you. Turn some of the energy that you use to support other people inward and use it for yourself.

Affirmation

I embody emotional balance, responding to challenges with grace and understanding.

Journal Prompts

★ Is there anyone you know that could use more support from you? How can you be more compassionate toward the people in your life?

★ How can you better manage and regulate your emotions?

★ What emotional healing or self-reflection do you need to prioritize?

CHAPTER 9

The Suit of Swords

"I think..."

Keywords

Intellect, thinking, decision-making, reason, truth, communication, conflict.

Understanding the Suit of Swords

In the tarot realm of Swords, the suit represents the sharp and cunning power of your mind, thoughts, and to be frank, your stupidity. Swords represent the ultimate tool for slicing through BS and illusions to get to the truth, while also sometimes slicing through the BS you may have created.

The Sword, which is double-edged, symbolizes the dual nature of your thoughts and your ability to use your thoughts to bring clarity to your situation or to create conflict and chaos. It is sharp enough to cut through the fog to get to the heart of the matter and serves as a reminder of the harm that our mismanaged thoughts can create. It is your responsibility to wield your thoughts and words with care and precision brought by the wisdom gained while navigating the Fool's Journey.

Swords represent the element of air and are the embodiment of having your head in the clouds. The mind often soars while thinking, daydreaming, and worrying, and without the proper fortitude will cause you to get swept up in the airy currents of the brain's natural chatter. Swords are also represented by the colors white or silver, symbolizing clarity and the purity that comes with truth.

The Swords suit is for the seekers of wisdom, and those brave enough to journey into the often-terrifying maze of the mind. This suit will highlight the journey of your intellectual pursuits, while teaching you about the power of your thinking. When Swords appear in a reading, it is offering you the opportunity to hone your mental prowess and embrace your inner wisdom.

Ace of Swords

A SHARPENED MIND

Astrological Associations

Celestial Body
Mercury

Zodiac Signs
Gemini, Libra, Aquarius

Keywords
Breakthrough, truth, clarity, logic, ideas, communication, decisiveness.

Understanding the Ace of Swords

The Ace of Swords depicts a cloud with a hand reaching out offering you an upright Sword. This is the sword of truth and an opportunity to strengthen mental clarity and experience fresh ideas. The hand extending from the cloud is a representation of Spirit giving you an offering of finding clarity in times of confusion. The crown is decorated with a laurel wreath, symbolizing a sharp idea that brings you victory. The golden raindrops are the Hebrew letter *Yod*, meaning the "finger of God," symbolizing that this is divine clarity.

Card Meaning

Eureka! The Ace of Swords is that "aha!" moment or the feeling of being struck by the lightning bolt of revelation. It is the razor-sharp sword of truth that slices through any BS that has been clouding your judgement. It represents an intellectual or mental breakthrough.

The Ace of Swords teaches you to seek the truth in all situations while embracing challenges with a sharp mind and mental prowess. It teaches you to be decisive, objective, and discerning.

Affirmation

With a sharp mind, I cut through any confusion present in
this situation.

Journal Prompts

★   What areas of your life could benefit from a fresh perspective?

★   What truths do you need to acknowledge and confront?

★   How can you effectively communicate your ideas and thoughts to others?

Two of Swords

MAKING AN OBJECTIVE DECISION

Astrological Associations

Celestial Body
Moon

Zodiac Sign
Libra

Keywords
Indecision, contemplation.

Understanding the Two of Swords

The Two of Swords depicts a blindfolded woman sitting on a bench, holding two swords crossed over her heart center. The swords represent the need for decision-making, and being crossed over her heart center symbolizes a lack of clarity that may be creating frustration or an emotional experience. Two swords symbolize that there are two choices to choose from. She sits at a quiet seaside, with the water suggesting the need to control emotions, be objective, and be impartial. The moon symbolizes her reliance on intuition and the blindfold signifies using her inner wisdom as a guide as opposed to relying on external influences. She is weighing her options.

Card Meaning

The Two of Swords represents indecision or being stuck in the "should I, shouldn't I" loop. It portrays a time of uncertainty or inability to choose and symbolizes the struggle of making a choice between two opposing or conflicting options.

The Two of Swords teaches you that to embrace the power of choice, you must first find the balance between your head and your heart.

Affirmation

I trust that the right path will reveal itself.

Journal Prompts

★ What major decisions are you currently facing in your life?

★ How do you typically approach decision-making? Is it with logic, emotion, or intuition?

★ How can you create a sense of inner peace prior to making important decisions?

Three of Swords

A SHOT TO THE HEART

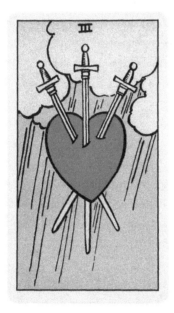

Astrological Associations

Celestial Body
Saturn

Zodiac Sign
Libra

Keywords
Heartbreak, disappointment, betrayal, sadness, pain, healing.

Understanding the Three of Swords

The Three of Swords depicts a heart pierced by three swords. The
swords represent the negative thoughts or memories associated with
a situation that caused emotional wounding and pain. The heart is
surrounded by clouds and rain during a storm. The clouds symbolize
mental anguish, and the rain represents the tears you cry when
experiencing heightened emotions.

Card Meaning

The Three of Swords represents heartache and emotional turmoil that
is triggered by loss, separation, or betrayal. It is that sharp shock to
the heart.

The Three of Swords teaches you to acknowledge your feelings to
begin the healing process and find closure. It is important to honor
your pain and sadness while allowing yourself to grieve. Do not worry;
this storm shall pass.

It may go without saying, but you probably do not want to see this card
appear in a relationship reading.

Affirmation

I honor my emotions and allow myself to grieve.

Journal Prompts

★ Reflect on past heartbreaks or betrayals. How did you
cope with the pain, and what lessons did you learn from
those experiences?

★ How do you typically handle difficult emotions? Are there
healthier ways you can express and release them?

★ What emotions are you currently avoiding or repressing?

Four of Swords

RECHARGING YOUR MENTAL BATTERIES

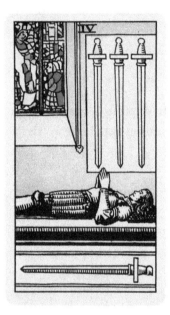

Astrological Associations

Celestial Body
Jupiter

Zodiac Sign
Libra

Keywords
Meditation, enlightenment, rest, recovery, funeral.

Understanding the Four of Swords

The Four of Swords depicts a knight who has returned from battle and is now lying on top of a casket in a church. He lies with his hands clasped above his chest in prayer. His swords are hung up above him, while one lies by his side. The hung swords represent moving on from a mental battle to prioritize peace. The coffin symbolizes the need for rest after a tough mental journey. The church and prayer hands suggest a time of introspection and reconciliation while communicating with the divine. He is reflecting on a stressful situation that heavily impacted him mentally.

Card Meaning

The Four of Swords represents taking the time to step away from the chaos of life to rest and recharge your mental batteries. It symbolizes that you are in a time of quiet introspection while prioritizing self-care following a difficult situation. This card is often known as the "meditation" card.

The Four of Swords teaches you the value of prioritizing your mental health by taking regular breaks for rest and rejuvenation. By giving yourself the gift of silence, you can gain valuable insights, find your inner peace, and prepare for what happens next in the Fool's Journey.

Affirmation

I honor my need for rest and rejuvenation.

Journal Prompts

★   Describe a time when you felt overwhelmed or mentally fatigued. How did you handle it, and did you allow yourself time to rest and recuperate?

★   What steps can you take to prioritize self-care and create a space for healing and recovery?

★   What activities can you incorporate into your life to add more
moments of stillness and mindfulness into your daily routine?

Five of Swords

WINNING AT THE EXPENSE OF OTHERS

Astrological Associations

Celestial Body
Venus

Zodiac Sign
Aquarius

Keywords
Conflict, confrontation, defeat.

Understanding the Five of Swords

The Five of Swords depicts a man holding three swords while two others lie on the ground. He stands in victory smirking while two other men walk away looking defeated. All the swords represent conflict, and the victorious man is symbolic of excelling at the expense of others. On the contrary, the two swords on the ground symbolize that not all battles are worth winning. The men walking away represent the consequences of not choosing battles wisely. The Fool must learn not to underestimate the mental fortitude of others.

Card Meaning

The Five of Swords represents the aftermath of conflict and confrontation. Do you see yourself as the victor in this situation or as the one who has lost? Did you lose, or did you give up?

The Five of Swords teaches you about the value of considering others before you act, or you risk ruining relationships with people that may be important to you. Winning an argument at the expense of a loved one is not worth it and asserting your dominance over others may come with consequences.

Affirmation

I choose to resolve conflicts with compassion and empathy.

Journal Prompts

★   Describe a time when your ego influenced your actions. What were the consequences of your behavior, and what could you have done differently?

★   Think about a situation where you felt triumphant at the expense of others. How could you have approached the situation with more empathy and compassion?

★   Consider a current conflict in your life. How can you find
    common ground and work toward a resolution that benefits
    everyone involved?

Six of Swords

FINDING YOUR PEACE

Astrological Associations

Celestial Body
Mercury

Zodiac Sign
Aquarius

Keywords
Moving forward, transition, healing, mental clarity, travel.

Understanding the Six of Swords

The Six of Swords depicts two people in a boat, one being a guardian and one being a child. There are six swords in the boat standing upright with the tips pointed down. A ferryman is steering the boat to the other side of a lake. One side of the lake has calm waters, and the other side of the lake is choppy. The guardian represents a caring person that supports you during difficult times and the boat is a safe vessel for transition. The ferryman helps souls transition from a turbulent state of choppy waters to a more serene place on calm shores.

Card Meaning

The Six of Swords is your ticket out of turbulent waters and represents choosing to move forward from a challenging time in your life that has created mental anguish and turmoil. It symbolizes moving toward peace and tranquility to find mental clarity and a more harmonious state of being.

The Six of Swords teaches you that transitions are normal and embracing this change with an open mind can help the healing process be less painful. It asks you to seek support when life gets tough and to trust the process. It is time to leave the mental baggage behind while you sail toward calmer waters.

Affirmation

I navigate life's transitions with grace.

Journal Prompts

★ What emotional baggage are you ready to leave behind and move on from?

★ How do you navigate transitions in your life, and how can you improve this process?

★ Who are the supportive people in your life who can help you through challenging times? If there are no supportive people, how can you cultivate creating your supportive community?

Seven of Swords

COMPROMISING INTEGRITY

Astrological Associations

Celestial Body
Moon

Zodiac Sign
Aquarius

Keywords
Sneaky, cunning, deception, strategy, calculated risk, theft, escape.

Understanding the Seven of Swords

The Seven of Swords depicts a sneaky man tiptoeing away from tents with five swords in hand, leaving behind two. His sneaky nature represents a need for stealth movement to outsmart others. He is being cunning and deceitful to commit an act of theft. As swords represent the mind, leaving two swords behind symbolizes making a strategic decision to take what is most important.

Card Meaning

Watch your back! The Seven of Swords represents sneaky and calculated actions to fulfill one's agenda. It can warn of people being deceitful and intentions that are self-serving and potentially harmful to you. On the contrary, the Seven of Swords can represent the need to be more strategic in your decision-making.

The Seven of Swords teaches you that sometimes employing cleverness is necessary to accomplish a goal, but one must be sure not to cross the ethical line. Remember to carefully consider all aspects of a situation while simultaneously upholding your boundaries. Watch out for shady people and trust your gut. If it feels off, it probably is.

Affirmation

I trust in my ability to outsmart obstacles.

Journal Prompts

★ Consider a time when you were deceitful to get what you want. Were you successful? Did you feel guilty? What did you learn from the situation?

★ Do you believe it is important to be honest 100 percent of the time? Why or why not?

★ What risks are you willing to take to achieve your desires?

Eight of Swords

LIMITING BELIEFS

Astrological Associations

Celestial Body
Jupiter

Zodiac Sign
Gemini

Keywords
Self-imposed limitations, fear, victim mentality, negative thoughts, mental blockage.

Understanding the Eight of Swords

The Eight of Swords depicts a blindfolded woman surrounded by eight swords stuck in the ground. The swords are arranged like a fence or prison she is trapped inside. She is tied up and unable to move and is standing with one foot in the water with the other foot on land. The blindfold and ties represent limited beliefs and an inability to see reality. The swords symbolize a mental barrier that has been created. There are no prison guards present signifying that the prison created is self-imposed. The placement of her feet is reminiscent of temperance and symbolizes the need to find a balance between her mental state and emotions.

Card Meaning

The Eight of Swords represents negative thinking and limited beliefs so strong that they have created a mental prison. You are trapped in a maze of your thoughts and are blinded by fear and self-doubt.

The Eight of Swords teaches that you have the power to change your perspective and free yourself from the constraints of low vibrational thinking. It is time to confront your fears and recognize that your biggest enemy is you. Because guess what? If you remove your blindfold, you will notice that the way out is right in front of you.

Affirmation

I release myself from self-imposed limitations.

Journal Prompts

★   What are the main fears that you possess that hold you back in life?

★   In what areas of your life do you feel trapped or restricted? Why?

★   What steps can you take to break free from your mental prison
     to move forward?

Nine of Swords

SLAYING YOUR NIGHTMARES

Astrological Associations

Celestial Body
Mars

Zodiac Sign
Gemini

Keywords
Overthinking, anxiety, worry, insomnia, nightmares.

Understanding the Nine of Swords

The Nine of Swords depicts a man sitting upright in bed. Presumably, he woke up in the middle of the night. He buries his face in his hands while being tormented by the nine swords hanging on the wall behind him. The swords represent his worries, fears, and negative thoughts. His mental turmoil keeps him up at night.

Card Meaning

Sweet dreams? More like night terrors! The Nine of Swords represents anxiety so intense it causes sleepless nights. It symbolizes overthinking due to worries, fears, and doubts.

The Nine of Swords teaches you that your mind can be your best friend and worst enemy. You must address your fears and acknowledge your anxiety even if you need to seek additional support. It is time to release the fears that have been holding you back.

Ask yourself, are your fears rooted in reality?

Affirmation

I release the grip of fear and anxiety from my mind.

Journal Prompts

★ What reoccurring worries or anxieties keep you up at night?

★ Are your fears based on real-life threats or are they assumptions?

★ What self-care practices can you implement to reduce anxiety and improve your quality of sleep?

Ten of Swords

HITTING ROCK-BOTTOM

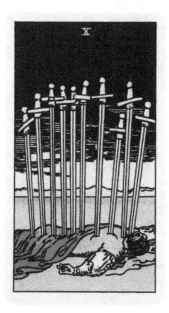

Astrological Associations

Celestial Body
Sun

Zodiac Sign
Gemini

Keywords
Rock-bottom, surrender, release, endings, transformation,
new beginnings.

Understanding the Ten of Swords

The Ten of Swords depicts a man lying face down. He has been stabbed in the back by ten swords. The dark sky of the night is fading as the bright sky of the day appears. The position of the man represents surrender or defeat. The ten swords symbolize the culmination of struggle, and the placement of the swords represents the pain caused by tumultuous mental situations. The sky signifies that there will always be a new day, and therefore, new beginnings.

Card Meaning

The Ten of Swords represents the end of a painful event that brought you to your knees. It is the culmination and end of a challenge. It signifies the release of the mental energy that created turmoil, which then ushers in a period of renewal.

The Ten of Swords teaches you that sometimes it is necessary to surrender for peace and closure. Endings are a natural part of life, and it creates room for a fresh start. Release that which no longer serves you, and trust that you are now walking out of the dark and into the brighter future that awaits you. Life may knock you down but you must always get back up.

Affirmation

I release the pain of the past, and like the sun, I still rise.

Journal Prompts

★   Reflect on a challenging experience. How has it shaped you as a person?

★   What patterns or behaviors can you leave behind to make space for growth and renewal?

★   In what ways can you turn this period of endings into an opportunity for new beginnings?

The Royal Family: Swords Court Cards

Swords Court Family Emblem

Butterfly

In the tarot, the butterfly is the universal symbol of transformation. It is a reminder to accept change with grace, as endings bring opportunities for growth and renewal.

The family emblem can be seen on the clothes and thrones of the Swords Court.

Astrological Associations

The Swords Court embodies all air signs—Gemini, Libra, and Aquarius.

Understanding the Swords Court

Welcome to the razor-sharp realm of the Swords Court cards! This is where intellect and quick wit reign supreme. This court delivers uncomfortable truths with brute honesty and directness.

In the Swords Court resides what I call the Royal Family of Swords, who rules over the mind, critical thinking, and decision-making, as well as the element of air. Like a fresh breeze, they bring a gust of mental energy to a reading. They also bring an *air* of authority—see what I did there?—regarding logic and rationality and have a mental acuteness capable of bringing clarity and insight to any situation. Think of them as the Board of Directors—the ultimate strategists.

Within this courtly family are characters who represent the essence of cleverness, sharp ideas, and clear and concise communication. They are powerful archetypes, guiding the Fool through the complicated mazes in the mind. The clarity brought by these cards encourages the Fool to challenge their fears, overcome worries, and embrace the power of the mind.

The Swords Court can represent actual people, such as family members, friends, or other people encountered in daily interactions. The cards can also represent people in certain professions, such as analysts, pilots, detectives, surgeons, lawyers, computer engineers, or other similar roles that require a substantial amount of mental fortitude.

With their swords, this court will slice up and dissect your problems faster than you can say the word "tarot." This court does not have room for being sentimental and instead tends to bury their emotions. They would rather dish out truth bombs that you may or may not be ready to hear. I hope you are ready for a reality check!

Page of Swords

SEEKER OF KNOWLEDGE

Keywords

Curiosity, learning, new ideas, communication.

Understanding the Page of Swords

The Page of Swords depicts a young girl holding a sword. She looks into the distance with a focused and inquisitive gaze. Her raised sword represents her sharp intellect and ability to find clarity during times of confusion. Her gaze symbolizes her curiosity and desire to explore what lies beyond the mountains behind her.

Card Meaning

The Page of Swords represents the beginning of new ideas and symbolizes new information being received. It is a time of being curious and signifies newfound opportunities to learn something new. The Page of Swords can also indicate incoming messages that require your discernment.

The Page of Swords teaches you to seek information, be inquisitive, and ask questions. This exploration leads to greater insights and a deeper understanding of your situation.

Affirmation

I welcome new opportunities for learning and growth.

Journal Prompts

★ What topics or areas of interest spark your curiosity the most?

★ Are there any limiting beliefs or fears that prevent you from asking questions when you do not know something? How can you overcome them?

★ Examine your communication style. What can you improve regarding how you communicate with others?

Knight of Swords

CHARGING AHEAD

Keywords

Assertiveness, impulsiveness, determination, pursuit, speed.

Understanding the Knight of Swords

The Knight of Swords depicts a determined knight on a horse quickly charging forward while raising his sword. The trees are blowing in the wind. His horse glances back at him with a look of concern. The raised sword represents his fearlessness as he cuts through obstacles and the swift movement symbolizes his decisiveness. The trepidation of the horse signifies that an idea has not been well thought out.

Card Meaning

The Knight of Swords represents being decisive in your pursuits and taking swift action to bring rapid progress. It is important not to sit on your goals and instead move toward them with determination. The Knight of Swords may also represent the need for using clear communication to bring you closer to fulfilling your dreams.

The Knight of Swords teaches you the importance of being proactive; however, it is still important to practice discernment. While it is nice to harness your inner trailblazer, the fast action of the Knight of Swords can make you a scatterbrain. Without proper discernment, you may realize you charged into battle but left your sword behind at the castle!

Affirmation

I take decisive action to achieve my dreams.

Journal Prompts

★   What is a specific goal or dream that you are determined to achieve? How can you take action to move closer to it?

★   Reflect on a time when you had to make a quick decision. How did it impact the situation, and what did you learn from it?

★   Are there any areas in your life where you need to be more assertive in your communication? How can you express yourself more confidently?

Queen of Swords

Keywords

Honesty, discernment, detachment, objective, fair, resolute.

Understanding the Queen of Swords

The Queen of Swords depicts a composed, regal woman sitting on a throne. She wears a robe adorned with clouds and holds a sword pointing upward. Her composed demeanor represents her ability to make calm and rational decisions. The sword in her hand symbolizes her ability to slice through illusions while being discerning. She is the only member of this court with clouds on their robe, which represents her ability to remain impartial while pursuing truth and justice, as she can still see when the view is obstructed.

Card Meaning

The Queen of Swords represents using intellect and objectivity to see situations clearly and make unbiased decisions.

The Queen of Swords teaches you the importance of maintaining mental clarity when examining a challenging set of circumstances and reinforces the need to be emotionally detached from some situations. It is a reminder to seek truth in the chaos.

Affirmation

I detach from my emotions to approach challenges with clarity and discernment.

Journal Prompts

★   Describe a time when you had to put your emotions aside to make a tough decision. What was the result? What did you learn from the experience?

★   Reflect on a situation where you had to be brutally honest with someone. How did they respond? How can you improve your communication techniques for the next time you have to be honest with someone?

★   Are there any areas where you would like to challenge yourself more mentally?

King of Swords

MASTER OF THE MIND

Keywords
Authority, intellect, logic, decisiveness, boundaries, communication.

Understanding the King of Swords
The King of Swords depicts a man with a commanding presence and a piercing gaze. He sits confidently on his throne while holding his sword upright. His sword represents his ability to analyze complex situations and make sound judgements. His commanding presence symbolizes his leadership and authority.

Card Meaning

The King of Swords represents the use of mastered intellectual capabilities to make fair and just decisions. It symbolizes a brainiac who is clear and sharp in communication.

The King of Swords teaches you the importance of the need to confidently take charge of situations, lead with logical thinking, and convey decisions made using clear and effective communication. Notice there is no water in this card, reminding you to prioritize your intellect prior to your emotions when tough decisions need to be made.

Affirmation

I inspire others with my vision and intellect.

Journal Prompts

★ Reflect on a time when you had to take charge of a situation due to someone else not leading effectively. What important decisions did you make? What can you do better?

★ Think of a conflict you resolved by using diplomacy and reason. How can you apply those skills to other areas of your life?

★ How well do you establish and maintain personal boundaries? Are there areas where you need to assert yourself more confidently?

CHAPTER 10

The Suit of Pentacles

"I have..."

Keywords

Money, possessions, material resources, career, business, property.

Understanding the Suit of Pentacles

Get ready to rise and grind as you journey through the prosperous (hopefully) tarot realm of the Pentacles suit. This is where you get to that bag, baby ("bag" means *money* for all my non-millennials) and experience the tangible pleasures that life has to offer. This suit is all about making that paper, building a foundation for your metaphorical castle, and indulging in the pleasures of life. Cha-ching!

The Pentacles are represented by the pentagram, which is then enclosed in a circle creating a pentacle. A pentagram is a five-pointed star, and each point of the star symbolizes spirit, water, fire, earth, and air. Enclosing this symbol in a circle represents bringing spirit and the elements together and pulling them down from the spiritual world and into the material. It is the embodiment of grounding your dreams into reality and manifesting your thoughts in the material world.

Pentacles represent the element of earth and symbolize possessions and material resources. Like tending to a garden, the Pentacles invite you to plant your seeds of abundance, nurture them through hard work, and watch them flourish while you reap the harvest. The colors green and brown also represents the Pentacles suit and is symbolic of the dirt from which thing grow and *money*, honey!

Ace of Pentacles

PLANTING SEEDS OF PROSPERITY

Astrological Associations

Celestial Body
Earth

Zodiac Signs
Taurus, Virgo, Capricorn

Keywords
Abundance, money, career, new opportunities, manifestation, tangible results.

Understanding the Ace of Pentacles

The Ace of Pentacles depicts a cloud with a hand reaching out,
offering you a pentacle. A path leads to a garden wall with an arch and
mountains in the distance. The outstretched hand represents a gift
from the universe, inviting you to seize the opportunity for prosperity.
The pentacle embodies the tangible rewards of your efforts and the
manifestation of your desires in the physical world. The pathway
leading to the arch symbolizes a gate to walk through as the Fool
begins a new earthbound journey.

Card Meaning

The Ace of Swords represents the physical manifestation of a new
opportunity or material gain. The Ace of Swords symbolizes turning
an idea into reality.

The Ace of Swords teaches you the importance of taking your dreams
and ambitions and grounding them into reality by practicing diligence.
It invites you to use the stability of earth energy and invest your time,
effort, and energy into projects that align with your long-term goals.

Affirmation

I am open to receiving abundance.

Journal Prompts

★   What are your most important material goals and aspirations?

★   What practical steps can you take to improve your
financial situation?

★   How can you transform your creative ideas into a
physical reality?

Two of Pentacles

THE BALANCING ACT

Astrological Associations

Celestial Body
Jupiter

Zodiac Sign
Capricorn

Keywords
Balance, adaptability, multitasking, priorities, financial decisions, juggling responsibilities.

Understanding the Two of Pentacles

The Two of Pentacles depicts a man juggling two large pentacles surrounded by a lemniscate (infinity symbol). He stands on the shoreline in front of a sea with turbulent waves. The man's ability to juggle the pentacles inside the lemniscate without dropping them represents his adaptability and resourcefulness while confronting life's infinite possibilities and ever-changing circumstances demonstrated by the sea's turbulent waves.

Card Meaning

The Two of Pentacles represents balancing financial matters as well as competing priorities. It symbolizes juggling all that life throws at you, including your work, managing finances, maintaining friendships, and caring for your family.

The Two of Pentacles teaches you to remain flexible through life's ebbs and flows. You will experience less resistance when you learn to embrace the chaos in all situations, laugh at its absurdity, and know that sometimes, dropping the ball (or pentacle) is another opportunity to learn how to master the art of balance. Remember, it is okay to fumble sometimes.

Affirmation

I flow with life's rhythm, juggling its challenges with grace and humor.

Journal Prompts

★ Consider the different roles you play in your life in work, family, and hobbies. How do you find the balance between them?

★ Are there any areas of your life where you feel like you are juggling too much? How can you find more equilibrium?

★ What tasks or responsibilities can you delegate to lighten your load?

Three of Pentacles

TEAMWORK MAKES THE DREAM WORK

Astrological Associations

Celestial Body
Mars

Zodiac Sign
Capricorn

Keywords
Collaboration, teamwork, apprenticeship, expertise, success.

Understanding the Three of Pentacles

The Three of Pentacles depicts a skilled craftsman standing on a workbench. He is using tools to build a cathedral and is being watched by two people—the client and the architect—holding a blueprint. They are observing the craftsman's work and providing feedback. The blueprint represents careful planning, which is needed for success, and the use of tools symbolizes expertise and precision while building the cathedral. The three figures are demonstrating teamwork while collaborating on a project.

Card Meaning

The Three of Pentacles represents being noticed publicly for your talents. It indicates being respected for your skill and expertise. The Three of Pentacles symbolizes recognizing the value of each person's work and contribution toward a project or goal.

The Three of Pentacles teaches you to observe and learn from others as this can refine your expertise. Embrace collaboration and pursue mentorship, as success can come to you through the contributions of others. Teamwork makes the dream work.

Affirmation

I recognize the value of combined efforts.

Journal Prompts

★ Are there areas in your life where you tend to take on tasks alone? How could you benefit from asking for help?

★ Describe a project or goal that you are currently working on. What areas could you involve others to improve the outcome?

★ Write about when you learned a valuable skill from someone who was more experienced than you. How did this experience help you grow?

Four of Pentacles

THE MISER

Astrological Associations

Celestial Body
Sun

Zodiac Sign
Capricorn

Keywords
Stability, security, control, possessiveness, hoarding, boundaries.

Understanding the Four of Pentacles

The Four of Pentacles depicts a man sitting on a bench guarding his four pentacles. He secures two large pentacles under his feet by stepping on them to prevent them from rolling away, balances a pentacle on his crown, and clutches a pentacle tightly in front of his chest. There is a city landscape in the background. His crown symbolizes that he has achieved success in the material world, but his tight grip on his pentacles represents a fear of losing what he has acquired or concern that his material possessions will be taken from him. The clutched pentacle in front of his heart center suggests his possessions are important to him. He has turned his back on the city behind him, signifying that he has shut out the world due to a lack of trust.

Card Meaning

The Four of Pentacles represents the accomplishment of or the desire to attain financial and material stability and security. It symbolizes the need for solidifying a firm foundation.

The Four of Pentacles teaches you that even though saving your earned resources to create a stable foundation may lead to security, allowing fear to drive your reason for saving may lead to hoarding. A part of the Fool's Journey is learning that even when you lose, you can always rebuild. If your hands are occupied holding on too tight to four pentacles, how will you hold ten of them?

Affirmation

I allow space for additional abundance to flow into the foundation I have already created.

Journal Prompts

★   What is your attitude toward money? How much does money define your sense of self-worth?

★ What material possession(s) are you holding onto tightly? Why is it so important to you, and what would happen if you let it go?

★ Consider a time when being frugal or saving money paid off. How did this affect your attitude toward financial security?

Five of Pentacles

FINANCIAL HARDSHIP

Astrological Associations

Celestial Body
Mercury

Zodiac Sign
Taurus

Keywords
Hardship, financial struggles, insecurity, survival mode, resilience.

Understanding the Five of Pentacles

The Five of Pentacles depicts two men trudging through the snow at night. They are wearing tattered clothing and rags and are not wearing shoes. One man is bandaged and walks while using crutches for support. They are walking in front of a church window that is being illuminated from the inside by a glowing, warm light. The bandaged man symbolizes being injured by life's challenges, and the tattered clothing and lack of shoes represent a loss of material resources. His crutches symbolize his need for outside support. The illuminated church is a representation of hope, community, and the support available to the men if they ask for help. It serves as a spiritual refuge during cold, dark times.

Card Meaning

The Five of Pentacles represents a loss of financial and material resources leading to challenging times. It symbolizes hardship.

The Five of Pentacles teaches you that even though you may experience hardship, being willing to seek help can ease the burden. Life is full of icy challenges that may make you feel left out in the cold, but you can weather any blizzard with the right attitude. It is okay to ask for support. You never know—you may end up with snow boots!

Affirmation

I am open to the support of others.

Journal Prompts

★ Describe a challenging time in your life when you felt financially strained. How did you cope with the situation, and what did you learn from that experience?

★ Consider the support systems you have in your life, be it friends, family, or community. How can you lean on them more during challenging times?

★ Write about a time when you helped someone out during a tough time. How did it make you feel, and what impact did it have?

Six of Pentacles

GIVING AND RECEIVING

Astrological Associations

Celestial Body
Moon

Zodiac Sign
Taurus

Keywords
Generosity, charity, giving, receiving, assistance.

Understanding the Six of Pentacles

The Six of Pentacles depicts a wealthy man giving coins to beggars. He holds a set of balanced scales. The beggars represent people who need resources. Resources can come in the form of money, but they can also be support, time, or information. The wealthy man bestowing coins symbolizes the empathy and understanding that people need when going through life's struggles. The balanced scale signifies using balance and fairness when considering how much to give and receive.

Card Meaning

The Six of Pentacles represents generosity, whether you are the one who is giving it or receiving it. It symbolizes using balanced discernment when giving to other people, as well as being smart when considering who to ask or accept additional support from.

The Six of Pentacles is a reminder that there is universal law, and that the universe operates using its own system of checks and balances. It teaches you to embrace the opportunities of sharing abundance or accepting needed assistance with grace. Everything in life is cyclical and, in that cycle, there will be times when you, the Fool, are helping others and times when you, the Fool, need help from others.

Affirmation

I accept assistance with grace and gratitude.

Journal Prompts

★ Explore your feelings about receiving help from other people. Are there any limiting beliefs that you hold that prevent you from accepting assistance when you need it?

★ Reflect on a time when you received unexpected assistance. How did it make you feel, and what impact did it have on your situation?

★   Describe a moment when you helped someone without
    expecting anything in return. How did that act of generosity
    influence your outlook on who you were as a person? How did
    it influence your outlook on life?

Seven of Pentacles

THE WAITING GAME

Astrological Associations

Celestial Body
Saturn

Zodiac Sign
Taurus

Keywords
Waiting, delayed gratification, evaluation, harvest.

Understanding the Seven of Pentacles

The Seven of Pentacles depicts a farmer leaning on a hoe and examining his pentacles hanging from a vine. The pentacles represent the fruits of his labor and the farmer's contemplative look symbolizes him taking stock of what has been achieved and what still needs to be done. His leaning on the hoe signifies him pausing to assess the progress of growth. He is determining if the seeds he has planted are growing the way he wants.

Card Meaning

The Seven of Pentacles represents assessing your current progress and determining whether it is time to harvest your crop. Are you observing the beginning of your manifestations, or do you need to provide more time for the seeds you have planted to grow? The Seven of Pentacles symbolizes taking a pause to evaluate your work.

The Seven of Pentacles teaches the importance of nurturing your ideas like how a farmer nurtures their crops. Success requires planting a seed, watering the garden, and trusting that the seed has enough intelligence to push through the dirt. Even though you cannot see what is happening beneath the soil, trust that your work is enough to produce a beautiful vine if given enough time.

Affirmation

My seed will sprout in divine time.

Journal Prompts

★ Imagine the fruits of your labor ripening on the vine. When considering your current goals, what does success look like?

★ Now that you have an idea of what success looks like for you, are your current actions in alignment with these goals, or is there a need for reassessment?

★ Reflect on a situation in your life where you feel that you are currently in a waiting period. How does this make you feel, and what lessons can you learn in this time of pause?

Eight of Pentacles

DUE DILIGENCE

Astrological Associations

Celestial Body
Sun

Zodiac Sign
Virgo

Keywords
Mastery, diligence, dedication, work ethic, focus.

Understanding the Eight of Pentacles

The Eight of Pentacles depicts a skilled artisan on a workbench diligently hammering the pentacles he is sculpting. There are completed pentacles hanging on a tree for people to admire and some pentacles on the ground that still need to be polished. The diligence of the artisan represents mastering your skills through dedication and focus. His commitment to hammering the pentacles symbolizes that he is putting time and effort toward honing his craft by hammering away at it.

Card Meaning

The Eight of Pentacles represents mastery and dedication toward your craft. It symbolizes embracing the grind and producing high-quality results through diligence and commitment. Stay focused and continue honing your skills as you are close to being noticed for your endeavors.

The Eight of Pentacles teaches you the importance of putting in the work if you want to see your efforts rise to success. It reminds you to focus on improving and perfecting your craft as you have the power to shape and sculpt your pentacles.

Affirmation

I am the master of my craft.

Journal Prompts

★ Explore your feelings and attitude toward hard work. Do you see it as a chore; if so, why? Or do you embrace the opportunity for growth and improvement?

★ Reflect on a skill or craft you want to develop. How do you currently approach improving this skill or craft?

★   Imagine the artisan's workshop as a metaphor for your life in the Fool's Journey. What aspects of your journey require dedication, focus, and refinement?

Nine of Pentacles

LAPPING IN LUXURY

Astrological Associations

Celestial Body
Venus

Zodiac Sign
Virgo

Keywords
Abundance, independence, self-sufficiency, achievement, luxury.

Understanding the Nine of Pentacles

The Nine of Pentacles depicts a woman standing in a well-tended, bountiful vineyard. The vines contain grapes and pentacles. She is dressed in a luxurious robe and a hooded falcon rests on her arm. A snail crawls in front of her. The vineyard represents the abundance that she has cultivated. The bounty of grapes and pentacles symbolize the fruits of her labor, or the rewards earned from focused and disciplined effort. So many rewards have been received, that not only can she enjoy the rewards, but she can also enjoy the luxuries provided by them. The falcon signifies intelligence, and the hood represents a disciplined mind, which is needed to prevent the unnecessary waste of the material resources gained. The snail suggests that her achievements have been gained through a slow and steady approach.

Card Meaning

The Nine of Pentacles represents reaching success and financial freedom. It symbolizes acknowledging your newfound autonomy gained from material achievements, as well as enjoying the luxuries of what has been earned.

The Nine of Pentacles teaches you not only to recognize the fruits of your labor but to *enjoy* the fruits of your labor. It is a reminder to explore your view of what you lack and acknowledge that your garden is currently in full bloom. Not only should you be sipping the wine you created in your vineyard, but you should also be savoring the essence of your hard work.

Affirmation

I allow myself to experience luxury.

Journal Prompts

★ Reflect on moments where you have come into abundance
    in your life. How did you respond? Did you allow yourself to
    experience it, or did you go into lack mode and hoard it?

★ Explore your relationship with your ability to be independent
    and self-sufficient. How comfortable are you in relying on
    yourself? What activities can you do to continue developing
    confidence in this part yourself?

★ Visualize a day of lapping in luxury. What does it look like,
    and how can you incorporate elements of that vision into your
    daily life?

Ten of Pentacles

CREATING YOUR LEGACY

Astrological Associations

Celestial Body
Mercury

Zodiac Sign
Virgo

Keywords
Material success, prosperity, fulfillment, inheritance, legacy.

Understanding the Ten of Pentacles

The Ten of Pentacles depicts a family of three generations: an elderly man, a couple, and a child. The elderly man sits on a small throne decorated with grapes and holds a long wand, and his robe is ornately adorned. They are at the front of the entrance to their property and their family crest hangs at the top of the arch. There are two dogs. The elderly man is reminiscent of the King of Pentacles at the end of his Fool's Journey. The length of his wand symbolizes the wealth of experience he has manifesting his goals into his physical reality. The large property represents material success and financial security, and the generational family and crest symbolize legacy and inheritance. The dogs act as guard dogs or spirit companions for the couple on their Fool's Journey (see the Fool).

Card Meaning

The Ten of Pentacles represents reaching the pinnacle of worldly success.

The Ten of Pentacles teaches you that the results of your hard work extend beyond just material resources, as it can also contribute to the resources that you can share with others. True abundance is more than money, it is also love, family, and community, which are all facets that make a full life.

Affirmation

I embrace the legacy that I create and inherit.

Journal Prompts

★ Explore your idea of worldly success. Beyond financial gain, what does true prosperity look like to you?

★   Imagine your ideal family life. What are some things you believe
    would contribute to a sense of abundance and fulfillment for
    you and your loved ones?

★   What is the legacy you want to leave behind? What are some
    habits you can create that will get you closer to this goal?

The Royal Family: Pentacles Court Cards

Pentacles Court Family Emblem

Grapes

In the tarot, grapes are associated with the element of earth and represent prosperity and fertility. Grapes grow in a cluster, allowing you to always harvest more than one piece of fruit. Even if one grape does not grow, there will still be others to eat, which symbolizes abundance.

The family emblem can be seen on the robe of the King of Pentacles and throughout the pentacles suit.

Astrological Associations

The Pentacles Court embodies all earth signs—Taurus, Virgo, and Capricorn.

Understanding the Pentacles Court

Welcome to the Court of Pentacles! The Royal Family of Pentacles rules the material realm while lapping in luxury. They have learned how to embrace and bask in the pleasures of the earthy realm, because why only manifest a tiny cottage when penthouses are houses too? A heated swimming pool? Yes, they will take that too. They are no strangers to getting their hands dirty by planting seeds and have perfected the method of nurturing their germinated sprouts into money trees.

This realm is where business and pleasures intermingle, and your dreams are manifested into the physical and transformed into dollar bills. This royal family governs material matters by exercising practicality, diligence, and responsibility, which helps to nurture steady growth. They provide us with the wisdom to navigate the material world to create a reality that feels secure and physically resourced.

The Pentacles Court can represent actual people, such as family members, friends, or other people encountered in daily interactions. The cards can also represent people in earthy professions that include finance or property, such as investors, bankers, accountants, property managers, realtors, and building contractors, as well as people who work with their hands such as craftsmen, woodworkers, or farmers. They can also represent people who make a lot of money, regardless of their profession.

If tangible results are what you want, then harness the grounded energy of the Pentacles Court. Over here, we do not chase dreams; we turn them into coins that jingle in our pockets.

Page of Pentacles

THE INTERN

Keywords

Manifestation, new beginnings, apprenticeship, study, practicality.

Understanding the Page of Pentacles

The Page of Pentacles depicts a young girl standing in a well-tended field with sprouting flowers. She is holding a pentacle and gazing at it with curiosity. She is learning about how to navigate earthly pursuits and achieve material success. The well-tended field represents new fertile ground, and the sprouting flowers symbolize that her ideas are about to bloom.

Card Meaning

The Page of Pentacles represents new beginnings in material pursuits. It symbolizes learning and exploring new monetary and practical aspects of life. It can indicate starting a new job, creating a new business, enrolling in a new course, or beginning a new project.

The Page of Pentacles teaches you that just when you think you know everything, there is always something new to learn. When manifesting, there is always another way to get your hands on what you want. Sometimes, you need to go back to the drawing board, approach the situation with a fresh, intern-like mind, and try something new.

Affirmation

I embrace my role as the cosmic intern.

Journal Prompts

★ What is that new job, business, course, or project that you are trying to pursue? What active steps can you take to bring you closer to that manifestation?

★ As we age, we sometimes become less curious due to thinking that we already understand the world. Contemplate your current relationship with the material world. How can you exercise wonder and curiosity in the everyday aspects of life?

★ Explore the concept of being a curious cosmic intern. How would you approach your earthly pursuits with an intern-like perspective? Could this add innovation to your pursuits?

Knight of Pentacles

THE WORKHORSE

Keywords

Responsibility, hard work, steady progress, methodical, grounded ambition.

Understanding the Knight of Pentacles

The Knight of Pentacles depicts a knight mounted on a horse. The horse is still and sturdy. The knight has leaves growing out of his helmet and the horse has leaves growing from its headdress. The stillness of the horse represents being contemplative and deliberate when making the next move. The leaves symbolize that the knight's ideas are beginning to materialize.

Card Meaning

The Knight of Pentacles represents making steady progress in your material pursuits. If you feel like progress has not been consistent, this card tells you to refine your plans and adopt a more methodical strategy for approaching your endeavors.

The Knight of Pentacles is a workhorse, and it teaches you that steady progress can come from hard work and meticulous planning. It reminds you that ambitions are often achieved through disciplined and consistent effort.

Affirmation

I know that every disciplined effort brings me closer to my goal.

Journal Prompts

★   Consider your long-term goals. What steps can you take today to lay the foundation for consistent, steady progress toward your future success?

★   Think about a previous goal or project that you worked on that did not turn out how you hoped. What methodical steps could you have taken to add to that goal or project's success?

★   Discipline may require hard work, but you should not sacrifice your well-being in the process. How can you incorporate more balance between your work and fun?

Queen of Pentacles

THE MATRIARCH

Keywords

Abundance, prosperity, generosity, nurturing, domestic, grounded.

Understanding the Queen of Pentacles

The Queen of Pentacles depicts a regal woman seated on a throne holding a pentacle in a field of blooming flowers. The throne is adorned with a goat head, cherubim, and pears. There is a rabbit at her feet. The goat head symbolizes Capricorn and represents practical, steadfast energy, the cherubs are angels that bring blessings, and the pears represent the fruits of her labor. The rabbit signifies luck, prosperity, and fertility. The blooming flowers symbolize all her manifestations.

Card Meaning

The Queen of Pentacles represents a time of prosperity, abundance, and fulfillment. It indicates good fortune and symbolizes coming into a windfall of material resources.

The Queen of Pentacles teaches you that not only are you creating your own abundance, but you are also *cultivating* it. Do not give up on your ideas and instead nurture them into fruition.

Affirmation

I manifest abundance by nurturing my ideas.

Journal Prompts

★   Think about areas of your life where people rely on you to be a nurturing provider. What can you do to improve your nurturing qualities?

★   Reflect on your role in your family and your community. How could you use the nurturing qualities from above to promote the growth of other people?

★   Think about things in your life that require practical attention. Could some of these things benefit from adopting a more nurturing approach?

King of Pentacles

THE TYCOON

Keywords

Wealth, success, materialism, stability, mastery, authority.

Understanding the King of Pentacles

The King of Pentacles depicts a man seated on a throne holding a
pentacle and a scepter. There are bulls carved into his throne. His
crown has a laurel wreath, and his robe is decorated with grape vines,
reminiscent of the robe the man wears in the Ten of Pentacles. He
sits in a lush, overgrown vineyard. Behind him is his house, a castle.
The pentacle represents him holding his prosperity and the scepter
symbolizes the power and authority he has in the material world. The
bulls represent Taurus and signify strength, power, and sacrifice. The

laurel wreath on his crown symbolizes victory and the overgrowth of grapes represents his affluence and achievements.

Card Meaning

The King of Pentacles represents material success, financial stability, and the achievement of goals. It indicates that your hard work has paid off and that you are in a time of abundance.

The King of Pentacles teaches you that it is possible to use your practical skills to build a kingdom. Use the methodical strategy you created and your ambition to harness tycoon energy. Soon, that foundation you built will turn into your castle.

Affirmation

I use the skills I have mastered to build my empire.

Journal Prompts

★   Examine the relationship you have with authority figures. How do you respond to authority, and how might this influence your leadership style?

★   If you struggle with authority, does this impact your ability to stand in your own authority? What are some steps you can take to heal your relationship with authority?

★   Explore the connection you have between patience and success in your life. Do you become impatient when trying to accomplish a goal? What are some areas where you can practice more patience?

Afterword

As we come to the end of the Fool's Journey through the tarot, I want
to extend my deepest gratitude to you, dear Fool, for allowing me
to join you on this adventure. Tarot is so much more than a tool for
divination; it is a pathway to self-discovery, a mirror reflecting the
depths of our souls, and a guiding light illuminating the path ahead.
As you continue to delve deeper into the world of tarot, remember to
embrace the journey with an open heart and mind. Whether you are a
seasoned tarot enthusiast or a curious beginner, I hope this book has
inspired and empowered you to explore the mysteries of the cards,
and if it was helpful, please leave a review on Amazon to help other
Fools find it!

May the wisdom of the cards serve as a beacon of guidance, leading
you to greater understanding and fulfillment in all areas of your life.
And may you always remember that the true magic of tarot lies not in
the cards themselves but in *you*.

About the Author

Meet Mystic Rainn, a mystical maven with a cosmic story that reads like an adventure traversing through the realms of spirit and space. She's a psychic medium, spiritual teacher, tarot reader, and reiki practitioner, and her unique gifts allow her to communicate with spirits and extraterrestrial beings. Yes, you read that right…aliens. She's like a cosmic conversationalist.

But Mystic Rainn's journey into the mystical arts was not exactly a straight path. As a child, she was what you might call an "airy fairy," with a tendency to astral project when boredom struck; however, she didn't know that was what she was doing. Instead, she called it "flying." She always had an intuition that surpassed her years, often knowing things that even adults couldn't think of. Back then, she didn't realize that her perspective of the world was anything out of the ordinary. She assumed everyone saw things the way she did, but as she got older, she realized many people didn't "see" at all.

It wasn't until she was thirteen years old that Mystic Rainn had her first confirmed encounter with the supernatural—a ghostly cat at a friend's house. Terrified by the experience, she made a conscious decision to shut off her ability to see spirits, and for the next seven years, she lived in blissful ignorance of the unseen world around her.

But then tragedy struck. At the age of twenty, Mystic Rainn's sister was brutally murdered, shattering her world in an instant. Suddenly thrust into a reality where the veil between the living and the dead was all too thin, Mystic Rainn's psychic abilities kicked into overdrive when she witnessed her dead sister stand outside of her lifeless body in the morgue. In the blink of an eye, she went from a regular college student to a full-blown psychic medium, navigating a world where the dead walked among the living.

As if that was not enough, just four months later, Mystic Rainn's mother passed away from a broken heart, forcing her gifts to open even wider. But amidst the chaos and grief, Mystic Rainn found a strength she never knew she had. She completed college early, earned not one but two master's degrees, and even graduated from law school.

Through it all, Mystic Rainn learned how to stand tall in the face of adversity, find her voice when others tried to silence her and chase after her dreams with unwavering determination. Her journey is a testament to the resilience of the human spirit and the transformative power of embracing the unknown.

In her quest for understanding and enlightenment, she turned to the tarot as a tool for self-discovery and guidance. What began as a personal journey soon blossomed into a calling, as Mystic Rainn discovered her innate ability to interpret the cards and offer profound insights to those seeking direction.

Today, Mystic Rainn is not only a skilled tarot reader but also a spiritual teacher, guiding others on their journeys of self-discovery and empowerment. With her unique blend of wisdom, intuition, and humor, she helps her clients unlock the secrets of the universe and embrace their true selves.

Mango Publishing, established in 2014, publishes an eclectic list of books by diverse authors—both new and established voices—on topics ranging from business, personal growth, women's empowerment, LGBTQ studies, health, and spirituality to history, popular culture, time management, decluttering, lifestyle, mental wellness, aging, and sustainable living. We were named 2019 *and* 2020's #1 fastest growing independent publisher by *Publishers Weekly*. Our success is driven by our main goal, which is to publish high-quality books that will entertain readers as well as make a positive difference in their lives.

Our readers are our most important resource; we value your input, suggestions, and ideas. We'd love to hear from you—after all, we are publishing books for you!

Please stay in touch with us and follow us at:

Facebook: Mango Publishing
Twitter: @MangoPublishing
Instagram: @MangoPublishing
LinkedIn: Mango Publishing
Pinterest: Mango Publishing
Newsletter: mangopublishinggroup.com/newsletter

Join us on Mango's journey to reinvent publishing, one book at a time.